Harvard Business Review

ON

GREEN BUSINESS STRATEGY

THE HARVARD BUSINESS REVIEW PAPERBACK SERIES

The series is designed to bring today's managers and professionals the fundamental information they need to stay competitive in a fast-moving world. From the preeminent thinkers whose work has defined an entire field to the rising stars who will redefine the way we think about business, here are the leading minds and landmark ideas that have established the *Harvard Business Review* as required reading for ambitious businesspeople in organizations around the globe.

Other books in the series:

Harvard Business Review Interviews with CEOs
Harvard Business Review on Advances in Strategy
Harvard Business Review on Appraising Employee Performance
Harvard Business Review on Becoming a High Performance Manager
Harvard Business Review on Brand Management
Harvard Business Review on Breakthrough Leadership
Harvard Business Review on Breakthrough Thinking
Harvard Business Review on Building Personal and Organizational Resilience
Harvard Business Review on Business and the Environment
Harvard Business Review on the Business Value of IT
Harvard Business Review on Change
Harvard Business Review on Compensation
Harvard Business Review on Corporate Ethics
Harvard Business Review on Corporate Governance
Harvard Business Review on Corporate Responsibility
Harvard Business Review on Corporate Strategy
Harvard Business Review on Crisis Management
Harvard Business Review on Culture and Change
Harvard Business Review on Customer Relationship Management

Harvard Business Review on Decision Making
Harvard Business Review on Developing Leaders
Harvard Business Review on Doing Business in China
Harvard Business Review on Effective Communication
Harvard Business Review on Entrepreneurship
Harvard Business Review on Finding and Keeping the Best People
Harvard Business Review on the High-Performance Organization
Harvard Business Review on Innovation
Harvard Business Review on the Innovative Enterprise
Harvard Business Review on Knowledge Management
Harvard Business Review on Leadership
Harvard Business Review on Leadership at the Top
Harvard Business Review on Leadership in a Changed World
Harvard Business Review on Leading in Turbulent Times
Harvard Business Review on Leading Through Change
Harvard Business Review on Making Smarter Decisions
Harvard Business Review on Managing Diversity
Harvard Business Review on Managing Health Care
Harvard Business Review on Managing High-Tech Industries
Harvard Business Review on Managing People
Harvard Business Review on Managing Projects
Harvard Business Review on Managing Uncertainty
Harvard Business Review on Managing the Value Chain
Harvard Business Review on Managing Your Career
Harvard Business Review on Managing Yourself
Harvard Business Review on Marketing
Harvard Business Review on Measuring Corporate Performance
Harvard Business Review on Mergers and Acquisitions
Harvard Business Review on the Mind of the Leader
Harvard Business Review on Motivating People

Other books in the series (continued):

Harvard Business Review on Negotiation and Conflict Resolution
Harvard Business Review on Nonprofits
Harvard Business Review on Organizational Learning
Harvard Business Review on Strategic Alliances
Harvard Business Review on Strategic Sales Management
Harvard Business Review on Strategies for Growth
Harvard Business Review on Supply-Chain Management
Harvard Business Review on Teams That Succeed
Harvard Business Review on the Tests of a Leader
Harvard Business Review on Top-Line Growth
Harvard Business Review on Turnarounds
Harvard Business Review on Women in Business
Harvard Business Review on Work and Life Balance

Harvard Business Review

ON

GREEN BUSINESS STRATEGY

A HARVARD BUSINESS REVIEW PAPERBACK

Printed in the United States of America
11 10 09 08 5 4 3

The *Harvard Business Review* articles in this collection are available as individual reprints. Discounts apply to quantity purchases. For information and ordering, please contact Customer Service, Harvard Business School Publishing, Boston, MA 02163. Telephone: (617) 783-7500 or (800) 988-0886, 8 A.M. to 6 P.M. Eastern Time, Monday through Friday. Fax: (617) 783-7555, 24 hours a day. E-mail: custserv@hbsp.harvard.edu.

Library of Congress Cataloging-in-Publication Data
Harvard business review on green business strategy.
p. cm. — (The Harvard business review paperback series)
ISBN-13: 978-1-4221-2108-5 (pbk. : alk. paper)
1. Industrial management—Environmental aspects. 2. Business enterprises—Environmental aspects. 3. Strategic planning—Environmental aspects 4. Social responsibility of business. I. Harvard business review. II. Title: Green business strategy.
HD30.255.H37 2007
658.4′083—dc22 2007030677

Contents

Harvard Business Review

ON

GREEN BUSINESS STRATEGY

Building the Green Way

CHARLES LOCKWOOD

Executive Summary

JUST FIVE OR SIX YEARS AGO, the term "green building" evoked visions of barefoot, tie-dyed, granola-munching denizens. There's been a large shift in perception.

Of course, green buildings are still known for conserving natural resources by, for example, minimizing on-site grading, using alternative materials, and recycling construction waste. But people now see the financial advantages as well. Well-designed green buildings yield lower utility costs, greater employee productivity, less absenteeism, and stronger attraction and retention of workers than standard buildings do. Green materials, mechanical systems, and furnishings have become more widely available and considerably less expensive than they used to be—often cheaper than their standard counterparts. So building green is no longer a pricey experiment; just about any company can do it on a standard budget by following the ten rules outlined by the author.

Reliable building-rating systems like the U.S. Green Building Council's rigorous Leadership in Energy and Environmental Design (LEED) program have done much to underscore the benefits of green construction. LEED evaluates buildings and awards points in several areas, such as water efficiency and indoor environmental quality. Other rating programs include the U.K.'s BREEAM (Building Research Establishment's Environmental Assessment Method) and Australia's Green Star.

Green construction is not simply getting more respect; it is rapidly becoming a necessity as corporations push it fully into the mainstream over the next five to ten years. In fact, the author says, the owners of standard buildings face massive obsolescence. To avoid this problem, they should carry out green renovations.

Corporations no longer have an excuse for eschewing environmental and economic sustainability. They have at their disposal tools proven to lower overhead costs, improve productivity, and strengthen the bottom line.

THE DRAMATIC, 647,000-square-foot PNC Firstside Center in downtown Pittsburgh boasts a magnificent facade of curving glass, steel, and stone overlooking the Monongahela River. The winner of several design awards, the building rises from a large plaza graced with waterfalls and fountains. Its airy, light-filled interior has 11-foot ceilings, floor-to-ceiling windows, an atrium, an open floor plan, and all the latest building system technologies, including individual climate controls. What most observers don't realize is that this is a "green," or environmentally and economically sustainable, workplace—and that it costs 20% less per square foot to operate than its comparably sized "standard" sister building in Philadelphia.

Green buildings, as many know, have less negative impact on the environment than standard buildings. Their construction minimizes on-site grading, saves natural resources by using alternative building materials, and recycles construction waste rather than sending truck after truck to landfills. A majority of a green building's interior spaces have natural lighting and outdoor views, while highly efficient HVAC (heating, ventilating, and air-conditioning) systems and low-VOC (volatile organic compound) materials like paint, flooring, and furniture create a superior indoor air quality.

Just five or six years ago, the term "green building" evoked visions of tie-dyed, granola-munching denizens walking around barefoot on straw mats as wind chimes tinkled near open windows. Today, the term suggests lower overhead costs, greater employee productivity, less absenteeism, and stronger employee attraction and retention. Companies as diverse as Bank of America, Genzyme, IBM, and Toyota are constructing or have already moved into green buildings. Green is not simply getting more respect; it is rapidly becoming a necessity as corporations—as well as home builders, retailers, health care institutions, governments, and others—push green buildings fully into the mainstream over the next five to ten years.

In fact, the owners of standard buildings face massive obsolescence. They must act now to protect their investments. "Building owners are starting to do reviews of their portfolios to see how green their buildings are and what they need to do to meet growing market demand," says Ché Wall, chair of the World Green Building Council. Citigroup, for example, has already begun looking at how its 100 largest buildings stack up against accepted green standards. Based on those findings, the company will then review its worldwide real estate portfolio and create a green road map to help improve the efficiency of its buildings. Soon, financial institutions and investors will use new valuation methodologies to quantify important green building factors like productivity and long-term life cycle costs when determining real estate values.

The Shift to Green

Before 2000, companies generally regarded green buildings as interesting experiments but unfeasible projects in the real business world. Since then, several factors have caused a major shift in thinking.

First, the creation of reliable building-rating and performance measurement systems for new construction and renovations has helped change corporate perceptions about green. In 2000, for example, the U.S. Green Building Council (USGBC) in Washington, DC, launched its rigorous Leadership in Energy and Environmental Design (LEED) rating program. LEED evaluates buildings and awards points in six areas, such as innovation and design process. The program has Certified, Silver, Gold, and Platinum award levels. Other rating programs include the UK's BREEAM (Building Research Establishment's Environmental Assessment Method) and Australia's Green Star. Certainly, companies can create green buildings without using these rating programs, and many that do follow program guidelines choose not to spend the time and money applying for certification.

Nevertheless, certification assures prospective buyers and tenants that a building is truly sustainable. (For more on these rating programs, see "Green Standards" at the end of this article.)

Second, hundreds of U.S. and international studies have proven the financial advantages of going green. Well-designed green buildings, for example, have lower utility costs. In its first year of operation, Genzyme Center—Genzyme Corporation's 12-story LEED-Platinum headquarters in Cambridge, Massachusetts—used 42% less energy and 34% less water than standard buildings of comparable size. Green buildings can also boost employee productivity by approximately 15%, in part because they use alternative building materials that don't emit toxins, like formaldehyde, that are commonly found in standard building materials and workplaces. At Genzyme Center, 58% of the 920 employees report that they're more productive there than they were in Genzyme's former headquarters building. Employee sick time in the new headquarters is 5% lower than for all of Genzyme's other Massachusetts facilities combined. Moreover, green design criteria—including abundant daylighting, individual climate controls, and outdoor views—raise morale and employee satisfaction, which also improves productivity.

Finally, green building materials, mechanical systems, and furnishings have become more widely available, and their prices have dropped considerably—in some cases below the cost of their standard counterparts. According to Turner Construction chairman Thomas C. Leppert, four industry studies of more than 150 sustainable buildings across the United States show that, on average, it costs only 0.8% more to achieve basic LEED certification than to construct a standard building. The PNC Firstside

Center was already under construction as a standard building when the owner, PNC Financial Services Group, decided to go green instead. Even so, the project was completed two months early, came in $4 million under the original (and only) construction budget, and earned LEED's Silver rating. Now, PNC has constructed several of more than 200 planned green bank branches. The average construction time was 45 days faster than for PNC's traditional branches, and the costs were the same or lower. In the northeastern United States, for example, PNC's green branches each came in $100,000 below the cost of a competitor's new standard branches.

Building green is no longer a pricey experiment; just about any company can do it on a standard budget by implementing the following ten rules.

Rule 1: Focus on the Big Picture

According to William Browning, a senior fellow at the Rocky Mountain Institute in Colorado, integrating green principles into a building's planning and design process can generate 40% more savings and 40% better performance than simply adding green technologies to a traditionally planned and designed facility. Planning, designing, and constructing a green building isn't like installing new signage or adding a design feature at the last minute. If a company wants to stay within a standard budget and reap the full benefits of a sustainable building, all development decisions from the start must be guided by a green mind-set.

To launch a successful green planning and design process, it's important to hire the right project team members: architects, engineers, contractors, and consultants who are knowledgeable about the broad spectrum of green design tools and technologies and who have experience planning and constructing a variety of green facilities. Team members who are unfamiliar with green will often resist any deviation from standard design principles, building materials, and construction processes. They will make mistakes on everything from the amount of insulation needed to the selection of interior components like nontoxic flooring, therefore limiting the building's sustainability and having a negative impact on the budget.

A collaborative green project team begins by examining the building site, the exterior and interior plans, and the budget—managing up front each planning decision's effect on the overall project. A green planning and design process was essential to the success of the nine-story, $112 million (in Australian currency) global headquarters for Lend Lease in Sydney, Australia. The company wanted the building to set a new benchmark for energy efficiency and indoor air quality to increase worker satisfaction and retention, but it insisted on a standard budget. Also, the city had imposed height and building density limits, so the building needed to have the greatest possible amount of usable space on each floor. One way the project team surmounted these challenges was by selecting a water-based, chilled beam air-conditioning system. Although it cost 30% more to install than a standard system, the water-cooled system was 30% more energy efficient and took up less room between ceilings and floors, leaving more usable space on each floor. The team reexamined all of the other planned elements as well. Replacing standard T-8 lamps, for example, with more energy efficient T-5 lamps (with smaller housing units) was another way to save space, which helped reduce materials and construction costs.

Rule 2: Choose a Sustainable Site

If a building or a business campus is going to be truly green, it cannot be constructed on prime farmland, parkland, a historic or prehistoric site, or the habitat of an endangered species, nor can it be built within 100 feet of wetlands. Ideal locations for sustainable development include in-fill properties like parking lots and vacant lots, redevelopment sites like rail yards, and remediated brownfields. By choosing such locations, companies avoid contributing to sprawl and the degradation of environmentally significant sites, often while being near services they need.

Genzyme Center earned its LEED-Platinum rating in part because of its location. The building stands on a remediated brownfield site (where a coal gasification plant once stood). It is adjacent to a power plant—something that might typically be considered a challenge because it means unattractive views for workers and visitors. Genzyme, however, turned the plant's proximity into an opportunity by piping the plant's "waste" steam into the center's HVAC system to warm the building in the winter and cool it (with two steam absorption chillers) in the summer. Adopting this steam system reduced the building's electrical requirements and energy costs, and those savings are reimbursing the company for the system's higher up-front capital costs.

The LEED rating program gives points to properties located within a quarter mile of bus lines and within half a mile of rail and subway lines. Genzyme Center is a five-minute walk from a mass-transit station. Approximately 25% of the building's 920 employees leave their cars at home.

Rule 3: Do the Math

To complete a successful green building on a standard budget, the project team must apply a cost/benefit analysis to each component before allocating funding. For instance, a green roof costs more than a standard roof to install, but it brings a larger return on investment because it lasts years longer and provides more benefits, particularly storm water management and lower energy costs. (See Rule 5 and Rule 8.)

When DPR Construction planned its green regional office in Sacramento, California, it used a proprietary software program called Ecologic3 to analyze the costs and benefits of each point in the LEED rating system for this building, as well as the costs to own and operate it. According to Ted van der Linden, DPR's director of sustainable construction, the company weighed each possible LEED credit against the overall $6.2 million budget, projecting the costs and benefits of each credit, as well as a ten-year return on investment. DPR found that approximately $85,000 of the $6.2 million would be spent on additional green up-front costs, including architecture and engineering design fees. Over the first ten years, however, the 52,300-square-foot office building will more than make up that $85,000 by generating $400,000 in operations savings.

Cost/benefit analyses should also incorporate the financial assistance, tax breaks, and other incentives that more and more cities, states, and utility companies offer to organizations that construct green buildings. Chicago, for example, awards floor area ratio (FAR) density bonuses for downtown buildings that have green roofs. Since 2000, New York State's Green Building Tax Credit has given deductions against a company's or developer's state tax bill for projects that meet specific sustainable requirements, like the under-construction Bank of America Tower in Manhattan. California's Savings by Design program—sponsored by four of the state's largest utility companies—provides design assistance and subsidies for energy efficient non-residential buildings.

Rule 4: Make the Site Plan Work for You

Site planning can minimize the amount of on-site infrastructure like roads and parking lots, reduce grading and other earthwork, limit erosion, maximize sediment control, and provide easy access to public transportation—all of which will earn LEED points, lower construction costs, and reduce the facility and infrastructure footprint. IBM Tivoli Systems, for example, has dedicated 70% (63 acres) of its 90-acre headquarters campus in Austin, Texas, to open space. The rest of the site has been designated for structures (up to eight office buildings and parking garages) and infrastructure.

One simple site-planning strategy that can reap significant benefits is building orientation. Consider interior lighting. Typically, it makes up 20% to 25% of an office building's direct energy use partly because heat generated by the lights leads to more air-conditioning. Building orientation, however, can create a daylit interior that needs much less artificial lighting, saving money both up front and over the long run. In locations commonly subject to winds, buildings can be oriented to capture the breezes through rooftop clerestories and other windows that provide cross-ventilation.

Rule 5: Landscape for Savings

Landscaping, particularly in suburban locations, is another cost-effective green tool. It is especially good at minimizing heat islands—the buildup of heat from sunlight pouring onto dark, nonreflective surfaces. West- and south-facing building walls, for example, often become heat islands. Covering them with green screens (metal lattices planted with vines or climbing flowers) will greatly reduce the heat island effect and minimize interior solar heat gain. Mature trees can shade building walls, roofs on low-rise buildings, roads, and parking areas.

A green roof landscaped with drought-tolerant grasses and plants also lessens the heat island effect. On a downtown building that is surrounded by many other buildings—each of which acts as a heat island—the impact can be dramatic. For example, studies show that Chicago City Hall's landscaped roof surface was, on average, 70 degrees cooler in the summer than the standard dark, heat-trapping roofs of nearby buildings, and the air temperature above the roof was 15 degrees cooler. A green roof also helps clean the air, serves as a wildlife habitat, and absorbs and filters rain that would otherwise flood storm drains and streets.

Rule 6: Design for Greater Green

Companies can use a wide variety of techniques to cost-effectively design a green building. A long and narrow building shape, for example, maximizes natural lighting and ventilation for workers. Locating fixed elements like stairs, mechanical systems, and restrooms at the building's core creates a flexible and open perimeter, which also allows daylight to reach work areas. Operable windows and skylights enable natural ventilation in temperate weather. Windows with low-E (low-emission) glazing minimize interior solar heat gain and glare.

The LEED-Platinum CII-Sohrabji Godrej Green Business Centre in Hyderabad, India—the greenest building in the world when it was completed in 2003, according to the USGBC—was given a circular design that brings sunlight to every part of the 20,000-square-foot building. During the day, artificial lighting is not used in 90% of the Green Business Centre. Thanks to its green design and energy efficient technologies, it uses 55% less energy than a standard building of similar size.

Rule 7: Take Advantage of Technology

Green building technologies help conserve and even generate energy. Companies can, for example, install motion-sensitive lighting sensors and individual climate controls in offices and at workstations. They can also purchase highly efficient HVAC systems that do not use chlorofluorocarbon-, hydrochlorofluorocarbon-, or halon-based refrigerants, which deplete the ozone and require more energy than green refrigerants (ones that are chlorine free, for instance). Again, such technologies cost more up front than standard building systems, but companies and developers can stay on a mainstream budget by taking advantage of the growing number of incentives and funding opportunities offered to companies installing building systems that save energy over the long run.

Advanced energy-conserving systems and many other green features took up almost $23 million (16%) of Genzyme Center's $140 million budget. (LEED-Platinum buildings are more costly than other green buildings because they are testing the new designs, technologies, and building materials that will become accepted components in the future.) Genzyme, however, expects the building's green components to generate a return on investment in ten years, in part through lower operating costs but primarily through increased productivity, longer employee retention, and less sick time.

Green facilities can also produce some of their own electricity with alternative technologies. The experimental green Wal-Mart Supercenter in Aurora, Colorado, has a 50-kilowatt wind turbine, natural gas microturbines, and photovoltaic systems attached to the rooftop clerestories.

Rule 8: Save and Manage Water

As water becomes scarcer and more expensive in many parts of the world, firms need to focus on conservation. They can install water-conserving irrigation systems and plumbing, waterless urinals (which are more sanitary than standard ones), and native and drought-tolerant landscape plants, and they can use recycled (not potable) water for landscaping needs.

Many jurisdictions have storm water management regulations that property owners must satisfy to limit the risk of flooding in heavy rain and reduce pollutants, like motor oil and fertilizer, that are swept into storm water. While an undeveloped site is able to absorb a significant amount of rainfall, impermeable surfaces like buildings and parking lots greatly increase the amount and speed of storm water flowing through and off the site, raising the risk of flooding. To address this problem, the Wal-Mart Supercenter in Aurora has two 400-foot-long tree-shaded bioswales (shallow canals lined with plants) in its parking lot that help slow and cleanse rainfall runoff from the parking lot and building roof and create an attractive pedestrian environment. Green roofs and man-made retention ponds and wetlands are other effective storm water management tools that can also beautify and add value to a property.

Rule 9: Use Alternative Materials

Green building materials create a healthier and safer workplace for employees. According to a 2002 study by the Indoor Environment Department at the Lawrence Berkeley National Laboratory in California, approximately 23% of U.S. office workers experience two or more sick building syndrome (SBS) symptoms—such as dizziness, nausea, and acute eye, nose, and throat irritation—in their workplaces annually. The same study found that the improved air quality generated by the use of green design, building materials, and technologies lowers SBS symptoms by 20% to 50%, while colds and influenza are reduced by 9% to 20% and allergies and asthma drop by 8% to 25%.

Many types of sustainable, nontoxic building materials are now readily available at reasonable prices. These include low- and zero-VOC paints, strawboard made from wheat (rather than formaldehyde-laced particle board), and linoleum flooring made from jute and linseed oil (rather than standard vinyl, which is packed with toxins). Materials like 100% recycled carpeting and heavy steel, acoustic ceiling tiles and furniture with significant recycled content, and soybean-based insulation often cost the same as or less than standard materials, and they have much less negative impact on the environment.

Rule 10: Construct Green

How you build is just as important as where and what you build. Achieving a superior indoor air quality, for example, starts during the construction process. By coordinating wet and dry activities, construction crews can avoid contaminating dry materials with moisture and making them breeding grounds for mold or bacteria. Mechanical ductwork can be protected from project site pollutants if it's sealed in the factory before shipment and kept sealed until it's installed.

Recycling construction waste is part of the green process that brings several benefits. First, the waste is not dumped in a landfill. Second, recycling costs are often much lower than landfill fees. Finally, by crushing the concrete and asphalt from a demolished facility and using it as structural fill for a new building on that site, a company can save hundreds of thousands of dollars because it doesn't have to ship that waste off-site and buy gravel for structural fill. LEED gives points to every project that recycles at least 50% of its construction debris. Many companies do more. The Genzyme Center contractor, for example, recycled over 90% of the project's construction waste.

Revamp and Refresh

As green goes mainstream, standard buildings will rapidly become obsolete and lose value. To avoid this problem, building owners should carry out green renovations. The LEED-CI program for commercial interiors offers guidelines to convert any standard workplace into a green building by generally following the same ten rules that apply to new construction, such as selecting alternative building materials. A green renovation can include everything from a new green roof to more efficient HVAC and lighting systems, enlarged existing windows, and low-VOC paints and flooring. The LEED-CI renovation of the 110,000-square-foot Puget Sound Energy corporate headquarters in downtown Bellevue, Washington, included more natural lighting and outdoor views, low-VOC interior finishes, lighting controls and sensors, and other energy efficient technologies that have improved worker satisfaction and saved the company $10,000 annually in energy costs. Citigroup is working with the USGBC to develop a streamlined process that will enable companies to earn LEED certification across entire real estate portfolios rather than applying for a LEED rating one building at a time.

THE GREEN FUTURE is here. Like the dramatic, occasionally unsettling, and ultimately beneficial transformations wrought by the introduction of electric lights, telephones, elevators, and air-conditioning, green building principles are changing how we construct and use our workplaces. Armed with the ten rules discussed above, corporations no longer have an excuse for eschewing sustainability—they have tools that are proven to lower overhead costs, improve productivity, and strengthen the bottom line.

Green Standards

A KEY CATALYST for moving green buildings into the mainstream was the development of reliable standards and evaluation criteria around the world. In 1990, the UK government pioneered the green standards movement when, at the request of the British real estate industry, it launched BREEAM–the Building Research Establishment's Environmental Assessment Method. BREEAM evaluates the environmental performance of a broad spectrum of new and existing UK buildings.

In 2000, the U.S. Green Building Council–a coalition of more than 6,000 real estate professionals, government and other nonprofit organizations, and schools–started its Leadership in Energy and Environmental Design (LEED) rating program. The program awards points in the following categories: sustainable site (14 possible points), water efficiency (five possible points), energy and atmosphere (17 possible points), materials and resources (13 possible points), indoor environmental quality (15 possible points), and innovation and design process (five possible points). Companies can earn points for everything from brownfield redevelopment to public transportation access. LEED has four award levels: Certified (26-32 points), Silver (33-38 points), Gold (39-51 points), and Platinum (52-69 points). A LEED-Gold building has 50% less negative impact on the environment than a standard building. A LEED-Platinum building has at least 70% less negative impact. Dozens of U.S. cities and several states now require that new and renovated public buildings satisfy LEED criteria.

More and more countries are creating their own green standards. The Green Building Council of

Australia, founded in 2002, synthesized BREEAM, LEED, and other environmental criteria into the Green Star rating system, which is specific to the Australian environment, building practices, and real estate markets. India's Green Building Council is developing a rating system that it hopes to launch by the end of the year.

Toyota's Green Acres

THE SOUTH CAMPUS EXPANSION of Toyota Motor Sales' headquarters in Torrance, California, "was a pivotal project for the green building movement, because it was such a myth buster," says S. Richard Fedrizzi, president and CEO of the U.S. Green Building Council. The largest facility in the United States to earn a LEED-Gold rating when it opened in 2003, the South Campus cost no more to build than a standard low-rise business campus in southern California.

Using a mainstream budget of $90 per square foot, architects from LPA in Irvine, California, designed 624,000 square feet of space in two three-story office buildings. Each building has a long, narrow footprint and a north-south orientation to maximize interior daylighting. The perimeter of each floorplate is ringed with glass-enclosed private offices. Over 90% of the building's occupants enjoy natural light and outdoor views.

Since March 2003, when employees moved in, the South Campus has delivered substantial overhead savings. The buildings' rooftop photovoltaic panels, combined with highly efficient air-handling units and gas-powered chillers, help to make the South Campus buildings 31% more energy efficient than the company's comparable Service Development Center building. In a region that imports most of its water, the South Campus consumes 60% less water on its 40-acre, drought-tolerant landscaped site than the typical turf-planted and sprinkler-watered business campus. Its use of recycled water for landscape irrigation, building cooling, and toilet flushing saves 20.7 million gallons of potable water a year.

The largest benefits have been reaped in internal operations. "Since moving onto the South Campus, we've had a very high retention rate, and we've seen increases in productivity and drops in employee absenteeism," says Sanford Smith, Toyota Motor Sales' corporate manager of real estate facilities. "Toyota Customer Services, for example, had a 14% decrease in absenteeism." The South Campus has become a "must stop" on the green building circuit. Officials from a hundred companies, organizations, and cities have toured the facility. Toyota has also shared its green workplace best planning practices with organizations such as Disney, the New York Times, and the U.S. Air Force.

International Green

GREEN BUILDINGS are hardly a U.S. phenomenon. In fact, several European countries, particularly the United Kingdom and Germany, have been constructing cutting-edge sustainable buildings for two decades. India also has some of the world's most advanced green buildings, including the CII-Sohrabji Godrej Green Business Centre in Hyderabad. The facility combines traditional Indian building techniques with green innovations such as two wind towers that make air-conditioning virtually redundant.

In June 2005, mayors from 50 large cities around the world met at the United Nations World Environment Day conference in San Francisco and signed the Urban Environmental Accords, which set out 21 sustainable-living actions for each city to complete by 2012. As part of the accords, the mayors pledged to mandate green rating standards for all new municipal buildings in their respective cities.

The World Green Building Council (WGBC), which was formed in 1999, is also spreading sustainability globally. It currently has nine members: green building councils representing Australia, Brazil, Canada, India, Japan, Mexico, Spain, Taiwan, and the United States. The WGBC is now working to help establish green building councils—a prerequisite for WGBC membership—in China, Germany, the United Arab Emirates, and the United Kingdom.

Originally published in June 2006
Reprint R0606J

What Every Executive Needs to Know About Global Warming

KIMBERLY O'NEILL PACKARD AND
FOREST L. REINHARDT

Executive Summary

THANKS TO THE DEVELOPMENT of the Kyoto Protocol–an international plan to limit carbon dioxide and other so-called greenhouse gases in the atmosphere–global warming is beginning to assume a prominent position on the agendas of business executives. The protocol underscores the consensus among scientists that climate change is a threat that must be taken seriously. It also sends the message that although weather patterns aren't going to change overnight, new regulations designed to curb climate change may themselves disrupt the flow of business.

Faced with such a complex problem, however, many executives have wondered where to begin. They naturally feel defensive about possible new regulations, have difficulty reckoning the likely costs, and are overwhelmed by the scientific details. But it's just not good business to hope the problem will go away.

A sensible way to start is by taking a close look at the risks–and the inevitable opportunities–associated with shifts in the weather, potential regulatory changes, and the battle over public opinion. Forward-looking companies in a range of industries, from energy to insurance to automobiles, are already seeking ways to mitigate the effects of the weather on their operations, shape any regulatory regime that governments may devise, and inform the public about their efforts to reduce the problems associated with climate change.

Companies that calculate the risks and opportunities effectively–as they would for any other part of the business–will be able to make wise investments that allow them to survive the coming storms.

THE POSSIBILITY that the earth's surface temperature is rising—permanently and significantly—caught the public's attention during the brutal summer of 1988. But it wasn't until December 1997 that global warming began to assume a prominent position on business executives' agendas. That's when representatives of 160 nations, convened by the United Nations in Kyoto, Japan, adopted a plan that would limit the amounts of carbon dioxide and other so-called greenhouse gases being released into the atmosphere. If ratified, the Kyoto Protocol would require industrial nations to dramatically reduce emissions of those gases by no later than 2012.

The protocol underscores the growing consensus among scientists that global climate change is a threat that must be taken seriously. While a few skeptics still question the evidence, most experts believe that human activity is contributing, at least in part, to an increase in the earth's average surface temperature. Scientists also agree that an increase of as little as two degrees Fahrenheit is likely to cause more severe storms, floods, and droughts and accelerate the spread of disease. Such catastrophes could devastate not only individuals and communities but also businesses and entire economies.

The Kyoto Protocol also sounded a second warning to business leaders, namely that new regulations designed to reduce the likelihood of climate change may themselves disrupt the flow of business. If large-scale reductions of emissions are mandated by law, many manufacturers will have to dramatically change the way they operate. They will also have to contend with shifts in demand, as energy-efficient products overtake those that have long been dominant. It's no wonder that business leaders at the most recent World Economic Forum in Davos, Switzerland, voted global climate change as the most pressing issue confronting the world's business community.

Faced with such a complex problem, however, many executives have wondered where to begin. They naturally feel defensive about possible new regulations and have difficulty reckoning the likely costs. And despite the body of scientific evidence that points to climate change, they find the actual details overwhelming. But it's not good business to hope the problem will go away.

A good place to start would be to look closely at the risks—and the opportunities—associated with shifts in the weather, potential regulatory changes, and the battle over public opinion. Some forward-looking companies in a range of industries, from energy to insurance to automobiles, are already seeking ways to mitigate the effects of the weather on their operations, shape any regulatory regime that governments may devise, and inform the public about their efforts to reduce the problems associated with climate change. Companies that calculate the risks and opportunities effectively—as they would for any other part of the business—will be able to make wise investments that allow them to survive the coming storms.

Bad Weather Ahead

Although unusual weather conditions may strike the casual observer as common these days (perhaps accounting for the popularity of the Weather Channel), most of the extreme changes associated with climate change have yet to emerge. Nevertheless, companies whose assets are directly affected by the weather must plan now for the potentially widespread and negative consequences of climate change.

Insurance companies, for instance, should adapt their predictive models to ensure that their prices are accurate and to prevent large financial losses due to payouts after unexpectedly severe storms. To value waterfront properties correctly, real estate companies will have to keep up with the latest thinking on changes in flood patterns. Agriculture companies may eventually have to invest heavily in new areas where the climate has warmed enough to make farming viable; at the same time, they may have to abandon some investments, such as crop storage facilities, in regions that have become too warm. Businesses that cater to tourists face a variety of worrisome scenarios. More frequent storms may depress demand for vacations in some tropical areas, while warmer or drier mountain weather may prove disastrous to ski resorts.

Companies with climate-dependent assets must find ways to manage the risks associated with changes in the weather. For some, risk management should include investing in acquiring better information. For example, because many scientists believe that climate changes will lead to more severe hurricanes, a consortium of insurance companies has created the Risk Prediction Initiative to analyze developments in hurricane patterns.

Swiss Re, a leading reinsurer, has a group of in-house specialists who track the latest research in climate change and identify emerging risks and trends. The information is critical to Swiss Re's success, since its ability to turn a profit depends on its skills in assessing and pricing risk. The stakes are high. Thomas Streiff, head of Swiss Re's environmental management unit, points out that a single hurricane smashing into Miami could do property damage worth $60 billion to $80 billion, of which about 50% would be covered by insurance. Overall economic loss could exceed $100 billion.

All companies that buy property insurance in areas where the weather has become more volatile will be affected by insurers' reassessments of risk. Streiff says customers don't necessarily have to worry that their coverage will be dropped, or even that premiums will skyrocket. Instead, he suggests, companies seeking insurance may be required to invest more in risk reduction, such as by constructing sturdier buildings.

For companies that sell seeds, risk management could mean developing crops that can deliver higher yields in drier conditions. For timber operations, it could mean spending more on fire and pest management—drier conditions increase the risk of fire and make young trees weaker and more vulnerable to insect attack.

Some companies may choose to adjust their portfolios of climate-dependent assets. For example, some property and casualty insurers are trying to reduce the amount of coverage they provide in disaster-prone coastal areas such as Florida. As some businesses abandon the playing field, however, others may replace them and charge the premium prices made possible by reduced supply.

Over the long term, companies in a variety of industries may see demand for their products shift as climate change affects more people. For example, if tropical diseases migrate into more industrialized nations—which is likely as temperatures become warmer at higher latitudes—pharmaceutical companies may see their markets expand. For example, the demand for products such as malaria medicines may shoot up in the industrialized world.

Anticipating Regulations

Although it may be decades before people in Munich or Minneapolis have to worry about tropical diseases, regulations designed to curb climate change are already being proposed. So in a business sense, at least, global warming is here, posing a threat to business as usual. For instance, it's likely that governments will impose additional taxes on fossil fuel consumption and require that cars and appliances use less energy.

Such regulatory programs will change asset values. As regulations push up energy prices, they'll reduce the value of some assets—fleets of trucks that get particularly low gas mileage, for example, and poorly insulated commercial buildings. They will also increase the value of goods and services as diverse as renewable-energy technology, process-control equipment, and telecommunications services—such as teleconferences—that substitute for transportation.

As government regulatory schemes start to take shape, companies should speak up. They should support programs that give them flexibility in deciding how to reduce emissions. A command-and-control approach—in which all sources would be required to make proportional reductions in carbon-dioxide emissions, regardless of the cost or difficulty—could cost six times as much as market-based solutions, according to the White House Council of Economic Advisers. Astonishingly, most businesses have not actively promoted market approaches as an alternative to command and control.

One market approach is to tax emissions of greenhouse gases. Companies could then decide if it's more efficient to pay the tax or invest in reducing emissions. But given the aversion to tax increases in the United States, this approach is probably not politically feasible. A more viable solution would be to set up a system of tradable permits, as the U.S. Congress did for sulfur dioxide in the 1990 amendments to the Clean Air Act. Under such a system, the government allocates emissions permits that companies can then buy and sell. Businesses that would have to pay huge sums to reduce their emissions of greenhouse gases could instead buy permits from companies that are able to make the required operating changes more cheaply. A tradable-permits system could reduce overall costs while giving businesses a continuing incentive to cut emissions.

Whatever regulatory systems emerge, some companies stand to make money from the changes. Makers of industrial process controls, like Honeywell and ABB, may be some of the big winners. They are already investing in sophisticated thermostats, equipment that generates electricity more efficiently, and other products and services whose value will increase in a world of higher-cost energy.

Agriculture and forest-products companies may also find new opportunities, especially if they can persuade governments to subsidize or otherwise encourage a variety of activities that remove carbon dioxide from the air. Planting trees may in some cases turn out to be a cheaper way to limit atmospheric carbon dioxide than reducing emissions, so companies that plant forests should lobby for regulations that recognize their efforts. Cultivation practices such as no-till agriculture can prevent the release of carbon dioxide into the atmosphere by reducing disturbance of the soil—and makers of herbicides that facilitate no-till agriculture will want to communicate that fact to policy makers.

It's easy to understand why companies that grow trees or make energy-efficient products might support new regulations. It's less clear, at first blush, why General Motors has advocated government policies that may make driving more expensive, such as reduced subsidies for fossil-fuel production. But the truth is, GM and other large automakers such as Ford see climate change as an opportunity to gain advantages over their less technologically sophisticated rivals. That's why they are investing in cars that run on a combination of gasoline and battery power and in fuel cells that combine hydrogen with oxygen to provide electricity without producing carbon dioxide. As the cost of driving conventional automobiles rises, Ford and GM may be able to dominate a new market and freeze out smaller competitors for whom the required investments would be too great.

Like automakers, energy companies stand to be hit hard by any new policies that arise from the anticipation of global climate change. The energy industry provides an illuminating contrast between a company that has adopted a forward-looking strategy and another that supports the status quo.

BP Amoco has been a leader in supporting international efforts to slow climate change. It has even announced voluntary cutbacks of its own carbon dioxide output, promising that its emissions of greenhouse gases in 2010 will be 10% below 1990 levels—even though the company expects its output and sales to be roughly 50% greater in 2010 than they were in 1990. BP Amoco's voluntary cutbacks are similar to those that would be required under the Kyoto Protocol. To help reach the announced goals, it has established an in-house carbon dioxide trading program that requires business units to buy and sell allowable emissions levels.

CEO John Browne and other BP Amoco executives do not expect retail customers to switch their business from other oil companies (at least in the short term), and they admit that they do not know exactly what the carbon-dioxide reductions will cost the company. But they are confident that their commitment is sensible. For one thing, they believe that taking a leadership position on climate change gives the company a distinctive identity in the eyes of government officials, scientists, and environmental groups. Such leadership may give BP Amoco better access to government-controlled oil deposits and more operating flexibility. Furthermore, the company's experiments with emissions trading are likely to give it clout at the negotiating table when international regulatory frameworks are being devised; company executives will be able to present hard data on how their system works.

BP Amoco's leaders also believe that by announcing the 10% cutback they'll release the creativity of employees and increase their commitment to the company. "Do not underestimate the power of preemptive, aspirational target setting," says Chris Gibson-Smith, BP Amoco's executive director for policy and technology. "The role of leadership is to invent actions that naturally have the consequence of transforming people's thinking." In other words, confronting the climate challenge will stimulate the company's employees—line workers and managers alike—to think more imaginatively. And to the extent that the employees see their values reflected in BP Amoco's goals, they may become more committed to their jobs and to the company. It's clear that this managerial approach has very little to do with conventional, engineering-driven ideas about pollution control.

On the other side of the divide is ExxonMobil. The company maintains that the evidence for global climate change is inconclusive and that no international accord is necessary. Unlike BP Amoco, ExxonMobil was until recently a member of the Global Climate Coalition, a consortium of trade groups in the energy business and other industries that oppose regulatory controls (the coalition no longer has individual companies as members). The coalition and its supporters appear to be betting against the weight of scientific opinion, but their approach to the problem may be subtler than it appears. If they can stall regulation of carbon-dioxide emissions, they might be able to protect the short-term values of their assets. They may hope they'll be able to convince the public that government regulation is a greater evil than climate change. In doing so, they run the risk of missing out on the opportunity to help tip the balance toward more sensible forms of intervention.

The Climate of Public Opinion

Probably the only thing more unpredictable than the weather is public opinion. But good publicity can pay big dividends: as the intensity and level of public interest increase, companies known to have made early efforts to tackle climate change will have seats at the negotiating table when regulations are being debated.

Although some companies are making investments to increase energy efficiency and to study and accommodate changes in weather patterns, most of those efforts have not reached the public's attention. Surprisingly few companies make public statements—or even have pages on their Web sites—about how they are dealing with climate change.

By contrast, Swiss Re has been vocal about its investments in knowledge on climate change, and the company has broadcast its concerns at industry conferences, on the Web, and in discussions with the insurers that are its customers. BP Amoco has also made public announcements about its commitment to reducing carbon-dioxide emissions, including a high-octane address by John Browne at Stanford in 1997 and other speeches. Further information can be found on company Web pages.

For strategic reasons, some companies have chosen to be quiet about their efforts. Makers of process controls like Honeywell and ABB would gain advantages from more stringent emissions regulations, but they've had to be cautious in their public statements on global warming. Some of their biggest customers are fossil fuel and electricity companies, and antagonizing those customers by taking a tough stance on regulations would be counterproductive.

While good PR buzz on preventing or preparing for climate change has its appeal, smart companies realize they have to earn the public's trust. They know it's simply bad business practice to make investments, relocate resources, or change strategies solely for the sake of appearance. They also realize that overstating their commitment to reducing global warming won't wash in the long run. The public will eventually see through pledges that are skin-deep. And losing the credibility needed to participate in future debates is a significant price to pay for a short-term public relations gain. That's why David Allen, who oversees BP Amoco's solar energy investments, is careful to emphasize that the company's foray into solar "is not just a public-relations sop. We would not do that. If you just paint something, then people will in due course see it as paint."

As they think through the PR challenges, executives should bear in mind the trade-offs between the pursuit of regulations with short-term advantages and the encouragement of a regulatory climate that will be stable and predictable—and therefore friendly to investment—over the long term. They should recall that, following World War II, the United States began pushing its partners down a long, uneasy path toward free trade. Fifty years later, the system is still imperfect, but trade is much freer and incomes are much higher than they would be if government leaders had not been patient and far-sighted back in 1949. Building a workable international system to manage climate change is not a one-shot, one-year project. Business leaders would do best to sell their elected representatives on a long-term approach to managing the effects of climate change.

No Excuses for Inaction

Global warming is a problem characterized by uncertainties. And in a world where even TV weather forecasters can't accurately predict rain or sun, business leaders might be forgiven for tending to more immediate problems and leaving climate-change efforts to the next generation.

But as with any other risk, the uncertainty is no excuse for inaction. The vast majority of scientists agree that we will face serious consequences if we fail to address the problem. Given the long time it takes for climate changes to occur, drastic short-term actions don't seem necessary. But dealing with climate change will be expensive. It may cost us as much as we have spent on cleaning up air and water pollution over the past three decades. Clearly, business leaders need to inform themselves about climate change and think systematically about its effects on their companies' strategies, asset values, and investments.

The ability to think steadily and consistently about a topic as complicated as climate change is a tough test of management acumen. Some executives are meeting it head-on. Those who are not should wonder why they aren't—and so should their shareholders.

What a Difference a Degree Makes

WHAT DIFFERENCE does a degree or two make? On a single spring day in Des Moines, Iowa, no one will notice much if the temperature goes from 68 degrees to 70 degrees. But when the average temperature across the planet rises–and stays at the higher level–the difference has enormous implications.

The Intergovernmental Panel on Climate Change, a scientific body convened by the UN, has developed models to predict changes to the global climate over the next 100 years. The IPCC projects an increase of two to six degrees Fahrenheit, which it says would likely have major effects on rainfall patterns and sea levels. Rainfall patterns would change because in a warmer climate both evaporation and precipitation, on average, would intensify. Climatologists also point out that the balance between winter and summer precipitation might shift, leading to increasingly frequent droughts in some areas. As a result, many more people will be at risk for flooding, and extended droughts could severely limit inland drinking water supplies. Sea levels would rise because ocean waters would expand as they became warmer.

Ecosystems would suffer if they couldn't change quickly enough to keep up with shifts in regional climates. The IPCC estimates that about one-third of the world's forests would undergo major changes in vegetation types. As forests changed, species that depended on them would become extinct.

Agriculture would face many changes. Some might be beneficial–for instance, the amount of arable land in the northern hemisphere could increase once potentially fertile areas in Canada and Siberia became warm enough for farming. On the other hand, higher temperatures can reduce yields of some crops, and agricultural pests now confined to warmer regions could invade temperate areas. Rising sea levels could significantly decrease the amount of low-lying land available for cultivation, especially in the developing world.

Some climate scientists assert that the overall effects of increased carbon dioxide levels would be beneficial; after all, plants use it to make the simple sugars on which the entire food chain depends. The assertion sounds appealing at first. And who in Chicago, Toronto, or Zurich hasn't wished for a little global warming while commuting to work in a snowstorm?

Unfortunately, there are several flaws with that kind of thinking. First, global climate change is likely to increase snowfall in some regions, not decrease it. Second, the optimists are assuming that the temperature will rise once and then remain at its new level. But if climate change occurs, it will likely occur continuously and at an accelerating rate. Moreover, our infrastructure investments fit the current climate: we have railroad and irrigation infrastructures where it now makes sense to grow crops, buildings designed to withstand the worst storms that are common to an area, ski lifts where it snows. If the climate changes, current investments will lose their value, and the costs of reinvesting elsewhere will be heavy.

The Greenhouse Effect

GREENHOUSE GASES have a bad reputation these days, but they've been warming the earth's climate for hundreds of millions of years. Without them, the earth's surface would be too cold to support life as we know it. The problem is that atmospheric concentrations of certain greenhouse gases have increased significantly over the past century. Here's how the process works.

The earth receives a tremendous amount of energy from the sun—a few days' worth of sunshine is equal to the amount of energy stored in all of the planet's fossil fuels. About 30% of solar radiation is reflected back into space; the rest is absorbed by oceans, land surfaces, clouds, and atmospheric gases, which then emit that energy in the form of thermal radiation. Naturally occurring greenhouse gases, especially water vapor and carbon dioxide, trap some of the thermal radiation and redirect it toward the earth's surface, insulating the earth like a blanket.

Human activity has increased the concentration of greenhouse gases in the atmosphere. At the same time, temperatures have increased. The warmer atmosphere is able to hold more water vapor, further enhancing the natural greenhouse effect.

Although carbon dioxide and other greenhouse gases, such as methane, are natural phenomena, human activity contributes significantly to the release of those gases into the atmosphere. Most man-made carbon dioxide comes from activities that involve the burning of fossil fuels, such as factory operations and driving. Deforestation also contributes to the greenhouse effect. Trees act as "sinks" for carbon dioxide—they absorb it from the atmosphere through photosynthesis. Burning this vegetation throws carbon dioxide into the air and reduces the quantity of sinks available.

Some greenhouse gases, including chlorofluorocarbons, are entirely artificial. Chlorofluorocarbons have also been implicated in the partial destruction of the stratospheric ozone layer, but ozone depletion and climate change are separate phenomena.

There is little doubt among scientists that the planet's climate will change if atmospheric concentrations of greenhouse gases continue to increase. The problem is pressing and real, and human activity is responsible for much of it.

The Kyoto Controversy

AT THE 1992 SUMMIT on the environment in Rio de Janeiro, diplomats pledged their nations to a voluntary program of reducing greenhouse gas emissions. A series of follow-up meetings culminated five years later in the Kyoto Protocol, a first attempt to put some teeth in the international regulatory framework. The protocol calls on industrial nations–it exempts developing countries–to reduce their emissions of greenhouse gases by specified percentages (using emissions levels in 1990 as a baseline) before deadlines ranging from 2008 to 2012.

The United States would have to reduce its emissions by 7%, the European Union by 8%, and Japan by 6%. Since the industrial world's economies are expected to grow over the next decade, the actual cutbacks required to meet the target are much greater–on the order of 35% to 50%.

The Kyoto Protocol has been attacked from all sides. Environmentalists see its demands as inadequate. Businesspeople and politicians decry the high costs it would impose and its short-term focus. Critics in the developed world denounce its exemption of nonindustrialized countries, pointing out that emissions from developing nations will soon surpass those from the industrial world. Leaders of developing countries counter that the rich countries got rich while greatly increasing their own emissions; why should developing countries be denied that option?

The protocol also looks very different to groups on opposite sides of the Atlantic. Ratification by the U.S. Senate appears unlikely, but European governments are going ahead as though the treaty had already been agreed upon; they will insist on credit for their early actions in negotiations over a final accord. Further, European governments tend to favor restricting nations from trading emissions reductions internationally; Americans generally oppose such restrictions.

In our view, the protocol deserves much of the criticism it has received. An improved framework could deliver more benefits to the environment at a lower cost. Flexibility, for example, needs to be built into any regulatory regime. While the protocol raised the possibility that countries could trade emissions allowances, it left the all-important details to be worked out later. It's critical that such trading be allowed. Why? Because countries that have lower energy efficiency will be able to reduce their emissions more cheaply–and therefore will have something to sell to more efficient countries, where reductions are harder to come by. Although the idea of "trading the right to pollute" sounds immoral to some, it encourages all participants to find the most efficient ways to reduce emissions. A global trading system for carbon dioxide would have the same wealth-increasing effects as global trading systems for other goods. It would enable the global community to reduce emissions where it can do so most cheaply–just as free markets concentrate production of wheat, oil, semiconductors, and software in places where those goods can be made at the lowest cost.

Countries also need flexible deadlines. Climate change is a long-term problem, and it would be better to get three tons of emissions reductions in 2020 than only one ton in 2010. Stretching out Kyoto's compliance schedules would also reduce the premature retirement of existing capital assets and thus drastically lower compliance costs.

Differences in perspective among the negotiating partners make agreements on climate change difficult. Whatever the fate of the Kyoto Protocol, the hard work of designing international regulations and institutions to address the climate change problem is just beginning. Companies should not stand by silently during this critical time.

Originally published in July–August 2000
Reprint R00409

Bringing the Environment Down to Earth

FOREST L. REINHARDT

Executive Summary

THE DEBATE ON BUSINESS and the environment has typically been framed in simple yes-or-no terms: "Does it pay to be green?" But the environment, like other business issues, requires a more complex approach–one that demands more than such all-or-nothing thinking. Managers need to ask instead, "Under what circumstances do particular kinds of environmental investments deliver returns to shareholders?"

This article presents five approaches that managers can take to identify those circumstances and integrate the environment into their business thinking. These approaches will enable companies with the right industry structure, competitive position, and managerial skills to reconcile their responsibility to shareholders with the pressure to be faithful stewards of the earth's resources.

Some companies can distance themselves from competitors by differentiating their products and commanding higher prices for them. Others may be able to "manage" their competitors by imposing a set of private regulations or by helping to shape the rules written by government officials. Still others may be able to cut costs and help the environment simultaneously. Almost all can learn to improve their management of risk and thus reduce the outlays associated with accidents, lawsuits, and boycotts. And some companies may even be able to make systemic changes that will redefine competition in their markets.

All five approaches can help managers bring the environment down to earth. And that means bringing the environment back into the fold of business problems and determining when it *really* pays to be green.

THE DEBATE ON BUSINESS and the environment has been framed in simplistic yes-or-no terms: "Does it pay to be green?" Many business school academics and environmental leaders have answered yes. Yet businesspeople are skeptical—and rightly so, since they instinctively reject such all-or-nothing thinking in other contexts: Does it pay to build your next plant in Singapore? To increase your debt-to-equity ratio? To sue your competitors for patent infringement? The answer, of course, is "It depends." And so it is with environmental questions: the right policy depends on the circumstances confronting the company and the strategy it has chosen.

Much of the writing about business and the environment ignores that basic point. The underlying assumption is that the earth is sick—and that therefore it *ought* to be profitable to find ways to help it return to good health. Promoting such causes and activities as recycling, solar energy, and small-scale agriculture should redound to business's benefit. But this is faulty reasoning. The truth is, environmental problems do not automatically create opportunities to make money. At the same time, the opposite stance—that it never pays for a company to invest in improving its environmental performance—is also incorrect.

That's why managers should look at environmental problems as business issues. They should make environmental investments for the same reasons they make other investments: because they expect them to deliver positive returns or to reduce risks. Managers need to go beyond the question "Does it pay to be green?" and ask instead "Under what circumstances do particular kinds of environmental investments deliver benefits to shareholders?"

I have identified five approaches that companies can take to integrate the environment into their business thinking. Some companies can distance themselves from their competitors by differentiating products and commanding higher prices for them. Others may be able to "manage" their competitors by imposing a set of private regulations or by helping to shape the rules written by government officials. Still others may be able to cut costs and help the environment simultaneously. Almost all of them can learn to improve their management of risk and thus reduce the outlays associated with accidents, lawsuits, and boycotts. And some companies may even be able to make systemic changes that will redefine competition in their markets.

The appeal of any of the five approaches will depend on the time horizon over which they are evaluated. As with other business problems, the environmental strategy that maximizes short-term cash flow is probably not the one that positions the company optimally for the long run. That's true of all business strategies in general, of course, but it especially applies to the environmental arena because benefits from environmental investments are often realized over long periods.

All of the approaches can help managers to bring the environment down to earth: to think systematically and realistically about the application of traditional business principles to environmental problems. They can enable some companies—those with the right industry structure, competitive position, and managerial skills—to deliver increased value to shareholders while making improvements in their environmental performance.

Differentiating Products

The idea behind environmental product differentiation is straightforward: companies create products or employ processes that offer greater environmental benefits or impose smaller environmental costs than those of their competitors. Such efforts may raise the business's costs, but they may also enable it to command higher prices, to capture additional market share, or both.

Consider an example from the textile industry. When textile manufacturers dye cotton or rayon fabric, they immerse the material in a bath containing dyes dissolved in water and then add salt to push the dyes out of the solution and into the cloth. Ciba Specialty Chemicals, a Swiss manufacturer of textile dyes, has introduced dyes that fix more readily to the fabric and therefore require less salt.

The new dyes help Ciba's customers in three ways. First, they lower the outlays for salt: textile companies using Ciba's new dyes can reduce their costs for salt by up to 2% of revenues—a significant drop in an industry with razor-thin profit margins. Second, they reduce manufacturers' costs for water treatment. Used bathwater—full of salt and unfixed dye—must be treated before it is released into rivers or streams (even in low-income countries where environmental standards may be relatively lax). Less salt and less unfixed dye mean lower water-treatment costs. Third, the new dyes' higher fixation rates make quality control easier, thus lowering the costs of rework.

Ciba's dyes are the result of years of development in the laboratory. They are protected against imitation by patents and by the unpatentable but complicated chemistry that goes into making them. For those reasons, Ciba can charge more for its dyes and capture some of the value it is creating for customers.

If this sounds like any other story about industrial marketing—add value to your customers' activities and then capture some of that value yourself—it should. Lowering a customer's environmental costs adds value to its operations just as surely as a new machine that enhances labor productivity does.

Three conditions are required for success with environmental product differentiation, and Ciba's approach satisfies all three. First, the company has identified customers who are willing to pay more for an environmentally friendly product. Second, it has been able to communicate its product's environmental benefits credibly. And third, it has been able to protect itself from imitators for long enough to profit on its investment.

If any of those three conditions break down, the product differentiation approach will not work. StarKist, the canned tuna subsidiary of H. J. Heinz, made this discovery when it decided to market dolphin-safe tuna.

Over the years, traditional techniques for catching tuna have caused the death of millions of dolphins. That's because the yellowfin tuna of the eastern tropical Pacific—the staple of tuna canners—often swim underneath schools of dolphin. A boat's crew would locate and chase a school of dolphins, drop a basketlike net under the school when the chase was over, and then haul in the tuna and the dolphins, often killing the dolphins in the process. Criticism of this practice, dating from the 1970s, intensified dramatically in 1989, when an environmental activist group released gruesome video footage of dolphins dying in the course of tuna-fishing operations.

In April 1990, StarKist announced that it would sell only tuna from the western Pacific, where tuna do not swim beneath dolphins. But the company ran into problems with all three conditions for success.

First, contrary to the company's survey findings that people would pay significantly more for dolphin-safe tuna, consumers proved unwilling to pay a premium for a cheap source of protein. It didn't help that western Pacific tuna was not yellowfin but skipjack, which people found inferior in taste.

Second, although StarKist made known its efforts to protect dolphins, it turned out that the fishing techniques practiced in the western Pacific were no environmental bargain. For each dolphin saved in the eastern Pacific, thousands of immature tuna and dozens of sharks, turtles, and other marine animals died in the western part of the ocean.

Finally, the company had no protection from imitators. Its main competitors, Bumble Bee and Chicken of the Sea, matched StarKist's move almost at once.

It would be easy to take from this story a universally gloomy message about the prospects for environmental product differentiation in consumer markets. Environmental quality, after all, is a public good: everyone gets to enjoy it regardless of who pays for it. From the standpoint of economic self-interest, one might wonder why any individual would be willing to pay for a public good.

But that view is too narrow. People willingly pay for public goods all the time: sometimes in cash, when they contribute to charities, and often in time, when they give blood, clean up litter from parks and highways, or rinse their soda bottles for recycling. The trick for companies is to find the right public good—or to offer an imaginative bundle of public and private goods—that will appeal to a targeted market.

For example, sellers of "designer beef"—meat from cattle that have not been exposed to herbicides or hormones—offer consumers potential health benefits (a private good) in addition to a more environmentally friendly product (a public good). And Patagonia, a California maker of recreational clothing, has developed a loyal base of high-income customers partly because its brand identity includes a commitment to conservation. Patagonia and the beef marketers have not only cleared the willingness-to-pay hurdle but have also found ways to communicate credibly about their products and to protect themselves from imitators through branding.

Managing Your Competitors

Not all companies will be able to increase their profits through environmental product differentiation. But some may be able to derive environmental and business benefits by working to change the rules of the game so that the playing field tilts in their favor. A company may need to incur higher costs to respond to environmental pressure, but it can still come out ahead if it forces competitors to raise their costs even more.

How can that be done? By joining with similarly positioned companies within an industry to set private standards, or by convincing government to create regulations that favor your product.

The first approach has been particularly successful in the chemical industry. In 1984, after toxic gas escaped from the plant of a Union Carbide subsidiary in Bhopal, India, and killed more than 2,000 people, the industry's image was tarnished, and it faced the threat of punitive government regulation. The industry recognized that it had to act—to forestall government regulations and improve its safety record without incurring unreasonable costs. As a result, the leading companies in the Chemical Manufacturers Association created an initiative called Responsible Care and developed a set of private regulations that the association's members adopted in 1988.

The U.S. companies that make up the CMA must comply with six management codes that cover such areas as pollution prevention, process safety, and emergency response. If they cannot show good-faith efforts to comply, their membership will be terminated. The initiative has enhanced the association's environmental reputation by producing results. Between 1988 and 1994, for example, U.S. chemical companies reduced their environmental releases of toxic materials by almost 50%. Although other industries were also achieving significant reductions during this period, the chemical industry's reductions were steeper than the national average.

Moreover, the big companies that organized Responsible Care have improved their competitive positions.

They spend a lower percentage of their revenues to improve their safety record than smaller competitors in the CMA; similarly, they spend a lower percentage of revenues on the monitoring, reporting, and administrative costs of the regulations. Finally, because the association's big companies do a great deal of business abroad, they have been able to persuade the CMA's foreign counterparts to initiate their own private regulatory programs—even in developing countries where one might expect little enthusiasm for tough environmental policies.

The prerequisites for the success of private regulatory programs like Responsible Care are the same as those for government regulatory programs. The regulators must be able to set measurable performance standards, have access to information to verify compliance, and be in a position to enforce their rules. Private programs also need at least the tacit approval of government: if they are incompatible with other rules such as antitrust laws, the private regulations won't hold up. And private regulations must cover all relevant competitors: it is no use for some companies to tie the hands of others if a third group has the potential to undercut them both.

The commodity chemicals business is better suited than most to private regulatory initiatives. Performance standards are comparatively easy to define because, for example, a perchloroethylene plant in Louisiana looks a lot like a perchloroethylene plant in New Jersey or Italy. Verifying compliance is not a problem either, because the companies constantly sell products to one another and thus can examine competitors' plants. Companies that violate the rules can be ousted from the association—even though it is illegal under antitrust law for the CMA to make compliance with Responsible Care a prerequisite for doing business with association members.

As an alternative to private regulation, companies that want to tie their competitors' hands can work with government regulators. Gasoline marketers in California followed this strategy when they helped design new state rules mandating reformulated gasoline to reduce air pollution.

Despite aggressive regulation in California in the 1970s and 1980s, many urban areas in the late 1980s were still not close to meeting national standards for smog, and regulators were threatening to require the use of methanol or ethanol fuels, or even to phase out gasoline-powered cars altogether. Rather than watch their markets erode, California gasoline refiners introduced reformulated gasolines containing a compound called methyl tertiary butyl ether (MTBE), and then gained regulatory mandates effectively requiring the use of these fuels.

The California gasoline refiners were in a strong position to use environmental regulation for strategic purposes. First, regulators were more than willing to act, given the state's ongoing smog problems. Second, the costs of the regulations would be spread among all of California's automobile drivers, so the chance of organized opposition was slight. Third, competitors from other states would have an even more difficult time selling in the California market. Outsiders already faced steep barriers to entry: pipeline capacity to California was limited, and the costs of transporting gasoline from, say, Texas were high. California's rules for reformulated gasoline erected another barrier and increased the collective pricing power of the California refiners.

Although the overall strategy was sound, the reformulated-gasoline policies have not been as effective as hoped. MTBE reduces air pollution, but leaks of the chemical have polluted groundwater. MTBE was found in municipal drinking-water wells in Santa Monica in 1997; it subsequently appeared in groundwater supplies elsewhere in the state. As a result, continued regulatory approval for MTBE use is now in jeopardy. Using environmental regulation strategically, as this example demonstrates, has both benefits and risks.

The approach of forcing rivals to match one's own behavior is fundamentally different from that of environmental product differentiation. A manager thinking about the choice between the two approaches needs to ask, Am I better off if my competitors match my investment or if they don't? If a company's customers are willing to reward it for improved environmental performance, the company will want to forestall imitation by competitors. But if its customers cannot be induced to pay a premium for an environmentally preferable good, then it may want its competitors to have to match its behavior.

Saving Costs

A third approach to reconciling shareholder value with environmental management focuses not on competitors but on internal cost reductions. Some organizations are able to cut costs and improve environmental performance simultaneously.

For instance, as many travelers know, major hotel chains over the past decade have tried to follow this approach. These companies' tactics include reducing their solid-waste generation and cutting their water and energy use. Many hotels have replaced small bottles of shampoo and lotion with bulk dispensers, saving money and reducing waste. One company saved nearly $37,000 per year after installing dispensers at a cost of $91,000.

Others use recycled packaging for amenities. Inter-Continental Hotels, for instance, reportedly saves $300,000 per year in this way at its ten properties in the United States and Canada.

Industrial companies have cut costs and enhanced environmental performance at the same time by redesigning inflexible or wasteful routines. Consider Xerox's efforts. After nearly three decades of market dominance, the company found its traditional markets crowded in the late 1980s with well-funded new entrants. Xerox's market share declined, and its margins eroded precipitously.

In 1990, the company's executives responded with a new management initiative—the Environmental Leadership Program—that eventually included waste reduction efforts, product "take-back" schemes, and design-for-environment initiatives. By the mid-1990s, Xerox's large manufacturing complex in Webster, New York, was sending only 2% of its hazardous waste to landfills. In the early 1990s, even before the program had a chance to bear much fruit, Xerox's executives were already labeling the program an unqualified success.

Xerox's story illustrates a common pattern: dramatic cost savings are often found when a company is under tremendous pressure. As long as Xerox was the unchallenged market leader, it could afford to be easygoing about cost savings—and it was. Yet when things got rough, it rose to the occasion with creative initiatives.

Observers of this pattern have wondered whether stringent environmental regulation could put the same kind of pressure on companies that competitive pressure does. They argue that "free" opportunities to improve environmental performance—in which the direct benefits to the company exceed the costs—are ubiquitous and that stricter regulatory requirements or changes in the tax code could force companies to uncover them. (For an example of such an argument, see "A Road Map for Natural Capitalism," by Amory B. Lovins, L. Hunter Lovins, and Paul Hawken, HBR May–June 1999.) Others disagree. They point out that managers are paid to minimize costs and wonder how adding new regulatory constraints could possibly reduce costs. Economists call this dispute the "free lunch" debate. The underlying issue is the appropriate level of government regulation.

The free lunch advocates overstate their case. Even low-hanging fruit can only be gathered after an investment of management time, and that resource is hardly free. Investments in environmental improvement, like all other investments, are worthwhile only if they deliver value after all the management costs have been included.

Fortunately, though, companies can remain agnostic on the question of whether free opportunities to improve environmental performance are widespread. From a business point of view, even if such opportunities are rare, managers should look for them as long as the search doesn't cost much in terms of their time or other resources.

Managing Environmental Risk

For many businesspeople, environmental management means risk management. Their primary objective is to avoid the costs that are associated with an industrial accident, a consumer boycott, or an environmental lawsuit. Fortunately, effective management of the business risk stemming from environmental problems can itself be a source of competitive advantage.

Alberta-Pacific Forest Industries, a Canadian venture of Japanese companies, has discovered that the voluntary provision of environmental goods can cost-effectively reduce long-term business risk. In 1993, the Japanese companies and their Canadian partners negotiated timber-harvesting rights on a vast tract of government-owned aspen and spruce forests in northern Alberta. The venture planned to build a conventional pulp mill that would use chlorine bleaching. It also planned to run the forests as they had always been run in western Canada, where, as one forestry manager put it, "There was never a plan for forest management, and 'forest planning' just meant 'fiber extraction.' "

But the project ran into a buzz saw of opposition from local farmers, aboriginal residents of northern Alberta, and environmental activists from around the world. Alberta-Pacific went back to the drawing board. It returned with plans for a mill that would keep pollution levels far lower than the government required; it also developed forest management policies that would substantially reduce traditional clear-cutting. In addition, it promised to hold regular public meetings, to communicate explicitly about the environmental impact of the company's operations, to carry out collaborative research with biologists from outside the company, and to provide recreational access to the woods.

The costs of these changes were modest and, in return, Alberta-Pacific improved its community relations and achieved more stable long-term costs. The changes are an insurance policy against regulatory difficulties, sour community relations, business interruptions, and related cost shocks. The leaders of Alberta-Pacific have realized that their ability to operate is contingent on society's approval, that the formal property rights they possess are necessary but not sufficient for them to cut timber and run mills, and that environmental improvements can make sense as risk management devices.

If Alberta-Pacific had not heeded the concerns of local residents and environmentalists, it likely would have been prohibited from using the land at all. And the stakes were high—the costs of raw materials were on a level one might find in Indonesia or Brazil, but the political and exchange-rate risks were far lower. The venture's small initial investments in the environment allowed it to profit from use of the forest.

Indeed, any company can benefit from an audit of its environmental insurance policies and risk management systems. Is the company buying the right policies? Is it retaining risk when the coverage is overpriced? Is it rewarding managers who reduce risk in their own operations or subsidizing risky behavior by failing to police it adequately?

Managers at Chevron are trying to answer those questions. They're analyzing the relative value of investing more in sprinkler systems, rapid response teams, maintenance, and other systems and activities that reduce environmental risk. They are also working to change employees' attitudes toward environmental and safety issues in order to reduce the risk of accidents. Chevron has found that environmental risk can be managed more effectively both by applying more rigorous quantitative analysis and by increasing its emphasis on training and cultural change programs.

It is not easy to prove that investments in environmental risk management are bearing fruit. And the potential for overinvestment is a concern. But just as it is for more traditional business risks, some investment in environmental risk management is prudent. (For a comparison of environmental and traditional risk management, see the insert "Integrating Risk Management.")

Redefining Markets

Some companies are following several approaches at once. In the process, they are rewriting the competitive rules in their markets.

As we've seen, Xerox has been a leader in searching for cost reductions. More dramatically, it has also attempted to redefine its business model. Rather than simply selling office equipment, it retains responsibility for the equipment's disposal, and it takes back products from customers when they are superseded by new technology. The machines are then disassembled, remanufactured to incorporate new technology, and resold at the same price as new machines. This practice enables Xerox to reduce its overall costs and also to make life difficult for competitors who lack similar capabilities. Customers benefit, too, because they no longer have to worry about the disposal of cumbersome machinery.

Rethinking traditional notions about property rights, as Xerox has done, is a useful way of discovering corporate opportunities to redefine markets based on environmental challenges. Instead of transferring all rights and responsibilities of ownership to their customers, Xerox and other manufacturers are retaining the obligation of disposal in return for control of the product at the end of its useful life.

Because of that initiative, Xerox reportedly saved $50 million in 1990, its first year. A drop in raw-materials purchases was the most significant component of the cost savings—fewer natural resources were used to make new machines. By 1995, Xerox estimated that it was saving more than several hundred million dollars annually by taking back used machines. Other manufacturers of electronic equipment such as Kodak, IBM, Canon, and Hewlett-Packard have undertaken similar initiatives.

Companies like Xerox that combine innovations in property rights and advances in technology may be able to create very strong competitive positions. Monsanto, DuPont, Novartis, and others are using this approach to redefine the agriculture industry. Instead of making traditional insecticides for crop pests, the companies transfer genetic material from naturally occurring bacteria to seeds so that the plants themselves become inedible to insects. These new seeds are highly profitable; they avoid the financial and environmental costs of making, transporting, and applying insecticides. But the path has not been free of rocks: environmental groups and consumers, especially in Europe, have protested the sale of genetically engineered products in their markets.

Like Xerox, Monsanto also redefined the property rights that go with its product. In order to recover its investment in seed technology, Monsanto needs repeat customers every year. But farmers commonly engage in a practice known as "brown bagging"—they save seeds left over from one year's crop to plant the following year. In return for the right to use the new type of seeds, Monsanto requires farmers to stop brown bagging and to submit to inspections to ensure compliance.

The ambitious strategies that Monsanto and Xerox are following have attracted a great deal of attention. But such strategies can entail significant market, regulatory, and scientific risks; they're not for every company—or even for every industry. The companies that appear to be succeeding are leaders in industries that face intensifying environmental pressure. Those companies have the research capabilities to develop new ways of delivering valuable services to their customers, the staying power to impose their vision of the future on their markets, and the resources to manage the inevitable risks. Moreover, by creating an appealing vision of a more profitable and environmentally responsible future, they may be better able to attract and retain the managers, scientists, and engineers who will enable them to build on their initial success.

Beyond All-or-Nothing

All-or-nothing arguments have dominated thinking about business and the environment. But it doesn't have to be that way. Consider how ideas about product quality have changed. At first, conventional wisdom held that improvements in quality had to be purchased at a cost of extra dollars and management attention. Then assertions were made that "quality is free": new savings would always pay for investments in improved quality. Now companies have arrived at a more nuanced view. They recognize that improving quality can sometimes lead to cost reductions, but they acknowledge that the right strategy depends on the company and its customers' requirements. It is time for business thinking on the environment to reach a similar middle ground.

As we've seen, environmental problems are best analyzed as business problems. Whether companies are attempting to differentiate their products, tie their competitors' hands, reduce internal costs, manage risk, or even reinvent their industry, the basic tasks do not change when the word "environmental" is included in the proposition.

Does all this mean that questions of social responsibility can be safely ignored? Not at all—but they're only one part of the equation. Companies aren't in business to solve the world's problems, nor should they be. After all, they have shareholders who want to see a return on their investments. That's why managers need to bring the environment back into the fold of business problems and determine when it *really* pays to be green.

Not all companies can profit from concern about the environment. Others will be able to do so by following one—and in some cases more than one—of the approaches described here. At any rate, a systematic look at environmental management opportunities is worth the time. Imaginative and capable managers who look at the environment as a business issue will find that the universe of possibilities is greater than they ever realized.

Beware of What You Know

TREATING ENVIRONMENTAL ISSUES as business problems sounds straightforward, but it's not easy. The following assumptions, all of which are common in business thinking, make it difficult to reframe the issues.

Environmental problems are, first and foremost, matters of social responsibility. While considerations of social responsibility are important, executives who frame environmental problems solely in those terms may overlook the business opportunities and risks that come with such problems. Treating environmental issues like other business issues can lead to more creative problem solving as well as better bottom-line results.

Environmental questions are cause for pessimism. In most arenas, successful managers search for opportunity in adversity and find in complex problems a chance to separate their companies from competitors. So it's striking to hear how passive and pessimistic they sound when talking about environmental issues. They take that approach because they associate it not just with extra costs but also with a loss of control over their own operations. But, as the examples in this article show, it doesn't have to be that way.

Environmental management is a zero-sum game. For every winner in a zero-sum contest, there is a loser. Thus if the environment wins, the company loses, and vice versa. That view is prevalent in part because it fits with the widespread perception that environmental problems are political or moral issues. Elections and crusades are win-lose by definition and by design, but businesses don't ordinarily operate that way. Instead, they look for chances to benefit themselves and others simultaneously. Some environmental problems are inevitably win-lose, but it's a mistake to think that none of them can be recast.

Government and environmental groups are the company's adversaries. At times, that view is justified; some regulators and advocates are indeed hostile to business. But government and nonprofit organizations will always play a role in environmental management—the only question is what kind of role. Sometimes it makes sense to circle the wagons against an external threat. But sometimes it makes sense for a company to ally itself with regulators or advocates against the competitors.

While managers must remain on guard against undue pessimism and passivity in dealing with environmental problems, they also need to beware of wishful or insular thinking that can intensify their environmental problems and cost their shareholders unnecessary money. These are some of the common pitfalls:

- ***Letting business interests sway your opinion of scientific and economic analysis.*** Managers shouldn't let the costs of solving an environmental problem affect their judgment of the scientific evidence that identifies the problem. Pulling the wool over your own eyes may convince you that you've averted disaster. In the long run, however, the fact that you can't see it doesn't mean you're hidden from danger.
- ***Assuming that maintaining the status quo is an option.*** It is common to use the status quo as a baseline–to look at the way things are today and to think about how you can change things on your own. But some change is likely to occur in any case, and managers need to be realistic about their ability to keep things as they are.
- ***Avoiding dissenting opinion.*** People find it comfortable to talk with those who share their views. Managers need to keep their minds open to the new perspectives and new facts that can come from regular conversations with government officials, environmentalists, and others outside their usual circle.

Those problems can all be overcome. If executives bring to environmental decision making the same kind of optimism, opportunism, analytic thinking, and openness that they instinctively bring to bear on other business problems, both their companies and the environment will benefit.

Integrating Risk Management

THINKING ABOUT ENVIRONMENTAL IMPROVEMENT as a risk management strategy, as managers at Alberta-Pacific and Chevron do, leads to the question, Should companies try to manage environmental risk in the same ways they manage other business risks?

In many companies, environmental risk is handled by the department that deals with environmental, health, and safety issues, while the management of currency and other financial risk is centralized under the treasurer or the financial officers. Those different parts of the organization usually take widely varying approaches to risk management and may even be ignorant of each other's activities.

There are legitimate reasons for managing environmental risk differently from other risks. Environmental risk is exceedingly difficult to assess quantitatively: no one can really know the probability of an accident occurring at a particular factory. By contrast, it's easier, say, to assess the probability that the dollar will move up or down against the yen—and market instruments exist that allow companies to hedge against such a risk.

Although it makes sense to manage environmental risk differently from other business risks, companies commonly make a serious mistake in the process: they rely too heavily on command-and-control mechanisms—in the form of procedural manuals and rules—to govern line managers' behavior. That approach impedes flexibility and fails to tap the expertise of individual line managers—the same problems that arise when government imposes command-and-control regulations.

Some reliance on command-and-control policies is probably necessary, but there are other ways to ensure effective risk management, and the wise risk manager uses a variety of approaches. A manager's environmental performance can be made a factor in determining incentive pay. Similarly, it can be considered in regular performance reviews and in the promotion process. And as information about environmental risks and their effects on a company's financials improves, it will become increasingly possible to handle environmental risk like other risks within the organization. For example, companies often buy insurance against environmental liability at the corporate level but don't charge operating managers for their unit's portion of the premiums. If they did, the managers' incentives would be better aligned with those of the company.

But even the steps outlined here will not change the inherently muddy nature of investments in environmental risk management. You can never be sure, even long after the fact, that investments designed to prevent an accident or a lawsuit were the right ones. That's why even sensible investments in risk management are extremely vulnerable to cost-cutting pressure. At the same time, the inability to determine measurable results can lead to overspending on risk reduction as well as to empire building in the environmental office.

To avoid such problems, senior managers need to ensure that those responsible for environmental risk are clear about the potential benefits of their investments. Managers whose responsibilities include environmental risk should be pushed to articulate why the level and type of investments they have chosen are appropriate. Furthermore, they need to communicate with those responsible for other sorts of business risk so that the approaches are consistent. That doesn't mean the approaches should be identical. Until managers have the same information about environmental risk as they have about currency risk, it won't make sense to manage the two in the same way—and that day is a long way off. But environmental risk management should not be shoved off to one side of the organizational chart and managed as a special case. Integrating it into the company's overall risk management approaches will yield better decisions over the long run.

Originally published in July–August 1999
Reprint 99408

A Road Map for Natural Capitalism

AMORY B. LOVINS, L. HUNTER LOVINS, AND PAUL HAWKEN

Executive Summary

NO ONE WOULD RUN a business without accounting for its capital outlays. Yet most companies overlook one major capital component–the value of the earth's ecosystem services. It is a staggering omission; recent calculations place the value of the earth's total ecosystem services–water storage, atmosphere regulation, climate control, and so on–at $33 trillion a year.

Not accounting for those costs has led to waste on a grand scale. But now a few farsighted companies are finding powerful business opportunities in conserving resources on a similarly grand scale. They are embarking on a journey toward "natural capitalism," a journey that comprises four major shifts in business practices.

The first stage involves dramatically increasing the productivity of natural resources, stretching them as much as 100 times further than they do today. In the second stage, companies adopt closed-loop production systems that yield no waste or toxicity. The third stage requires a fundamental change of business model—from one of selling products to one of delivering services. For example, a manufacturer would sell lighting services rather than lightbulbs, thus benefitting the seller and customer for developing extremely efficient, durable lightbulbs. The last stage involves reinvesting in natural capital to restore, sustain, and expand the planet's ecosystem.

Because natural capitalism is both necessary and profitable, it will subsume traditional industrialism, the authors argue, just as industrialism subsumed agrarianism. And the companies that are furthest down the road will have the competitive edge.

ON SEPTEMBER 16, 1991, a small group of scientists was sealed inside Biosphere II, a glittering 3.2-acre glass and metal dome in Oracle, Arizona. Two years later, when the radical attempt to replicate the earth's main ecosystems in miniature ended, the engineered environment was dying. The gaunt researchers had survived only because fresh air had been pumped in. Despite $200 million worth of elaborate equipment, Biosphere II had failed to generate breathable air, drinkable water, and adequate food for just eight people. Yet Biosphere I, the planet we all inhabit, effortlessly performs those tasks every day for 6 billion of us.

Disturbingly, Biosphere I is now itself at risk. The earth's ability to sustain life, and therefore economic activity, is threatened by the way we extract, process, transport, and dispose of a vast flow of resources—some

220 billion tons a year, or more than 20 times the average American's body weight every day. With dangerously narrow focus, our industries look only at the exploitable resources of the earth's ecosystems—its oceans, forests, and plains—and not at the larger services that those systems provide for free. Resources and ecosystem services both come from the earth—even from the same biological systems—but they're two different things. Forests, for instance, not only produce the resource of wood fiber but also provide such ecosystem services as water storage, habitat, and regulation of the atmosphere and climate. Yet companies that earn income from harvesting the wood fiber resource often do so in ways that damage the forest's ability to carry out its other vital tasks.

Unfortunately, the cost of destroying ecosystem services becomes apparent only when the services start to break down. In China's Yangtze basin in 1998, for example, deforestation triggered flooding that killed 3,700 people, dislocated 223 million, and inundated 60 million acres of cropland. That $30 billion disaster forced a logging moratorium and a $12 billion crash program of reforestation.

The reason companies (and governments) are so prodigal with ecosystem services is that the value of those services doesn't appear on the business balance sheet. But that's a staggering omission. The economy, after all, is embedded in the environment. Recent calculations published in the journal *Nature* conservatively estimate the value of all the earth's ecosystem services to be at least $33 trillion a year. That's close to the gross world product, and it implies a capitalized book value on the order of half a quadrillion dollars. What's more, for most of these services, there is no known substitute at any price, and we can't live without them.

This article puts forward a new approach not only for protecting the biosphere but also for improving profits and competitiveness. Some very simple changes to the way we run our businesses, built on advanced techniques for making resources more productive, can yield startling benefits both for today's shareholders and for future generations.

This approach is called *natural capitalism* because it's what capitalism might become if its largest category of capital—the "natural capital" of ecosystem services—were properly valued. The journey to natural capitalism involves four major shifts in business practices, all vitally interlinked:

- **Dramatically increase the productivity of natural resources.** Reducing the wasteful and destructive flow of resources from depletion to pollution represents a major business opportunity. Through fundamental changes in both production design and technology, farsighted companies are developing ways to make natural resources—energy, minerals, water, forests—stretch 5, 10, even 100 times further than they do today. These major resource savings often yield higher profits than small resource savings do—or even saving no resources at all would—and not only pay for themselves over time but in many cases reduce initial capital investments.

- **Shift to biologically inspired production models.** Natural capitalism seeks not merely to reduce waste but to eliminate the very concept of waste. In closed-loop production systems, modeled on nature's designs, every output either is returned harmlessly to the ecosystem as a nutrient, like compost, or becomes an input for manufacturing another product. Such systems can often be designed to eliminate the use of toxic materials, which can hamper nature's ability to reprocess materials.

- **Move to a solutions-based business model.** The business model of traditional manufacturing rests on the sale of goods. In the new model, value is instead delivered as a flow of services—providing illumination, for example, rather than selling lightbulbs. This model entails a new perception of value, a move from the acquisition of goods as a measure of affluence to one where well-being is measured by the continuous satisfaction of changing expectations for quality, utility, and performance. The new relationship aligns the interests of providers and customers in ways that reward them for implementing the first two innovations of natural capitalism—resource productivity and closed-loop manufacturing.
- **Reinvest in natural capital.** Ultimately, business must restore, sustain, and expand the planet's ecosystems so that they can produce their vital services and biological resources even more abundantly. Pressures to do so are mounting as human needs expand, the costs engendered by deteriorating ecosystems rise, and the environmental awareness of consumers increases. Fortunately, these pressures all create business value.

Natural capitalism is not motivated by a current scarcity of natural resources. Indeed, although many biological resources, like fish, are becoming scarce, most mined resources, such as copper and oil, seem ever more abundant. Indices of average commodity prices are at 28-year lows, thanks partly to powerful extractive technologies, which are often subsidized and whose damage to natural capital remains unaccounted for. Yet even despite these artificially low prices, using resources manyfold more productively can now be so profitable that pioneering companies—large and small—have already embarked on the journey toward natural capitalism.[1]

Still the question arises—if large resource savings are available and profitable, why haven't they all been captured already? The answer is simple: scores of common practices in both the private and public sectors systematically reward companies for wasting natural resources and penalize them for boosting resource productivity. For example, most companies expense their consumption of raw materials through the income statement but pass resource-saving investment through the balance sheet. That distortion makes it more tax efficient to waste fuel than to invest in improving fuel efficiency. In short, even though the road seems clear, the compass that companies use to direct their journey is broken. Later we'll look in more detail at some of the obstacles to resource productivity—and some of the important business opportunities they reveal. But first, let's map the route toward natural capitalism.

Dramatically Increase the Productivity of Natural Resources

In the first stage of a company's journey toward natural capitalism, it strives to wring out the waste of energy, water, materials, and other resources throughout its production systems and other operations. There are two main ways companies can do this at a profit. First, they can adopt a fresh approach to design that considers industrial systems as a whole rather than part by part. Second, companies can replace old industrial technologies with new ones, particularly with those based on natural processes and materials.

IMPLEMENTING WHOLE-SYSTEM DESIGN

Inventor Edwin Land once remarked that "people who seem to have had a new idea have often simply stopped having an old idea." This is particularly true when designing for resource savings. The old idea is one of diminishing returns—the greater the resource saving, the higher the cost. But that old idea is giving way to the new idea that bigger savings can cost less—that saving a large fraction of resources can actually cost less than saving a small fraction of resources. This is the concept of expanding returns, and it governs much of the revolutionary thinking behind whole-system design. Lean manufacturing is an example of whole-system thinking that has helped many companies dramatically reduce such forms of waste as lead times, defect rates, and inventory. Applying whole-system thinking to the productivity of natural resources can achieve even more.

Consider Interface Corporation, a leading maker of materials for commercial interiors. In its new Shanghai carpet factory, a liquid had to be circulated through a standard pumping loop similar to those used in nearly all industries. A top European company designed the system to use pumps requiring a total of 95 horsepower. But before construction began, Interface's engineer, Jan Schilham, realized that two embarrassingly simple design changes would cut that power requirement to only 7 horsepower—a 92% reduction. His redesigned system cost less to build, involved no new technology, and worked better in all respects.

What two design changes achieved this 12-fold saving in pumping power? First, Schilham chose fatter-than-usual pipes, which create much less friction than thin pipes do and therefore need far less pumping energy. The original designer had chosen thin pipes because, according to the textbook method, the extra cost of fatter ones wouldn't be justified by the pumping energy that they would save. This standard design trade-off optimizes the pipes by themselves but "pessimizes" the larger system. Schilham optimized the *whole* system by counting not only the higher capital cost of the fatter pipes but also the *lower* capital cost of the smaller pumping equipment that would be needed. The pumps, motors, motor controls, and electrical components could all be much smaller because there'd be less friction to overcome. Capital cost would fall far more for the smaller equipment than it would rise for the fatter pipe. Choosing big pipes and small pumps—rather than small pipes and big pumps—would therefore make the whole system cost less to build, even before counting its future energy savings.

Schilham's second innovation was to reduce the friction even more by making the pipes short and straight rather than long and crooked. He did this by laying out the pipes first, *then* positioning the various tanks, boilers, and other equipment that they connected. Designers normally locate the production equipment in arbitrary positions and then have a pipe fitter connect everything. Awkward placement forces the pipes to make numerous bends that greatly increase friction. The pipe fitters don't mind: they're paid by the hour, they profit from the extra pipes and fittings, and they don't pay for the oversized pumps or inflated electric bills. In addition to reducing those four kinds of costs, Schilham's short, straight pipes were easier to insulate, saving an extra 70 kilowatts of heat loss and repaying the insulation's cost in three months.

This small example has big implications for two reasons. First, pumping is the largest application of motors, and motors use three-quarters of all industrial electricity. Second, the lessons are very widely relevant. Interface's pumping loop shows how simple changes in design mentality can yield huge resource savings and returns on investment. This isn't rocket science; often it's just a rediscovery of good Victorian engineering principles that have been lost because of specialization.

Whole-system thinking can help managers find small changes that lead to big savings that are cheap, free, or even better than free (because they make the whole system cheaper to build). They can do this because often the right investment in one part of the system can produce multiple benefits throughout the system. For example, companies would gain 18 distinct economic benefits—of which direct energy savings is only one—if they switched from ordinary motors to premium-efficiency motors or from ordinary lighting ballasts (the transformer-like boxes that control fluorescent lamps) to electronic ballasts that automatically dim the lamps to match available daylight. If everyone in America integrated these and other selected technologies into all existing motor and lighting systems in an optimal way, the nation's $220-billion-a-year electric bill would be cut in half. The after-tax return on investing in these changes would in most cases exceed 100% per year.

The profits from saving electricity could be increased even further if companies also incorporated the best off-the-shelf improvements into their building structure and their office, heating, cooling, and other equipment. Overall, such changes could cut national electricity consumption by at least 75% and produce returns of around 100% a year on the investments made. More important, because workers would be more comfortable, better able to see, and less fatigued by noise, their productivity and the quality of their output would rise. Eight recent case studies of people working in well-designed, energy-efficient buildings measured labor productivity gains of 6% to 16%. Since a typical office pays about 100 times as much for people as it does for energy, this increased productivity in people is worth about 6 to 16 times as much as eliminating the entire energy bill.

Energy-saving, productivity-enhancing improvements can often be achieved at even lower cost by piggybacking them onto the periodic renovations that all buildings and factories need. A recent proposal for reallocating the normal 20-year renovation budget for a standard 200,000-square-foot glass-clad office tower near Chicago, Illinois, shows the potential of whole-system design. The proposal suggested replacing the aging glazing system with a new kind of window that lets in nearly six times more daylight than the old sun-blocking glass units. The new windows would reduce the flow of heat and noise four times better than traditional windows do. So even though the glass costs slightly more, the overall cost of the renovation would be reduced because the windows would let in cool, glare-free daylight that, when combined with more efficient lighting and office equipment, would reduce the need for air-conditioning by 75%. Installing a fourfold more efficient, but fourfold smaller, air-conditioning system would cost $200,000 less than giving the old system its normal 20-year renovation. The

$200,000 saved would, in turn, pay for the extra cost of the new windows and other improvements. This whole-system approach to renovation would not only save 75% of the building's total energy use, it would also greatly improve the building's comfort and marketability. Yet it would cost essentially the same as the normal renovation. There are about 100,000 twenty-year-old glass office towers in the United States that are ripe for such improvement.

Major gains in resource productivity require that the right steps be taken in the right order. Small changes made at the downstream end of a process often create far larger savings further upstream. In almost any industry that uses a pumping system, for example, saving one unit of liquid flow or friction in an exit pipe saves about ten units of fuel, cost, and pollution at the power station.

Of course, the original reduction in flow itself can bring direct benefits, which are often the reason changes are made in the first place. In the 1980s, while California's industry grew 30%, for example, its water use was cut by 30%, largely to avoid increased wastewater fees. But the resulting reduction in pumping energy (and the roughly tenfold larger saving in power-plant fuel and pollution) delivered bonus savings that were at the time largely unanticipated.

To see how downstream cuts in resource consumption can create huge savings upstream, consider how reducing the use of wood fiber disproportionately reduces the pressure to cut down forests. In round numbers, half of all harvested wood fiber is used for such structural products as lumber; the other half is used for paper and cardboard. In both cases, the biggest leverage comes from reducing the amount of the retail product used. If it takes, for example, three pounds of harvested trees to produce one pound of product, then saving one pound of product will save three pounds of trees—plus all the environmental damage avoided by not having to cut them down in the first place.

The easiest savings come from not using paper that's unwanted or unneeded. In an experiment at its Swiss headquarters, for example, Dow Europe cut office paper flow by about 30% in six weeks simply by discouraging unneeded information. For instance, mailing lists were eliminated and senders of memos got back receipts indicating whether each recipient had wanted the information. Taking those and other small steps, Dow was also able to increase labor productivity by a similar proportion because people could focus on what they really needed to read. Similarly, Danish hearing-aid maker Oticon saved upwards of 30% of its paper as a byproduct of redesigning its business processes to produce better decisions faster. Setting the default on office printers and copiers to double-sided mode reduced AT&T's paper costs by about 15%. Recently developed copiers and printers can even strip off old toner and printer ink, permitting each sheet to be reused about ten times.

Further savings can come from using thinner but stronger and more opaque paper, and from designing packaging more thoughtfully. In a 30-month effort at reducing such waste, Johnson & Johnson saved 2,750 tons of packaging, 1,600 tons of paper, $2.8 million, and at least 330 acres of forest annually. The downstream savings in paper use are multiplied by the savings further upstream, as less need for paper products (or less need for fiber to make each product) translates into less raw paper, less raw paper means less pulp, and less pulp requires fewer trees to be harvested from the forest.

Recycling paper and substituting alternative fibers such as wheat straw will save even more.

Comparable savings can be achieved for the wood fiber used in structural products. Pacific Gas and Electric, for example, sponsored an innovative design developed by Davis Energy Group that used engineered wood products to reduce the amount of wood needed in a stud wall for a typical tract house by more than 70%. These walls were stronger, cheaper, more stable, and insulated twice as well. Using them enabled the designers to eliminate heating and cooling equipment in a climate where temperatures range from freezing to 113°F. Eliminating the equipment made the whole house much less expensive both to build and to run while still maintaining high levels of comfort. Taken together, these and many other savings in the paper and construction industries could make our use of wood fiber so much more productive that, in principle, the entire world's present wood fiber needs could probably be met by an intensive tree farm about the size of Iowa.

ADOPTING INNOVATIVE TECHNOLOGIES

Implementing whole-system design goes hand in hand with introducing alternative, environmentally friendly technologies. Many of these are already available and profitable but not widely known. Some, like the "designer catalysts" that are transforming the chemical industry, are already runaway successes. Others are still making their way to market, delayed by cultural rather than by economic or technical barriers.

The automobile industry is particularly ripe for technological change. After a century of development, motorcar technology is showing signs of age. Only 1% of the energy consumed by today's cars is actually used to move the driver: only 15% to 20% of the power generated by burning gasoline reaches the wheels (the rest is lost in the engine and drivetrain) and 95% of the resulting propulsion moves the car, not the driver. The industry's infrastructure is hugely expensive and inefficient. Its convergent products compete for narrow niches in saturated core markets at commoditylike prices. Auto making is capital intensive, and product cycles are long. It is profitable in good years but subject to large losses in bad years. Like the typewriter industry just before the advent of personal computers, it is vulnerable to displacement by something completely different.

Enter the Hypercar. Since 1993, when Rocky Mountain Institute placed this automotive concept in the public domain, several dozen current and potential auto manufacturers have committed billions of dollars to its development and commercialization. The Hypercar integrates the best existing technologies to reduce the consumption of fuel as much as 85% and the amount of materials used up to 90% by introducing four main innovations.

First, making the vehicle out of advanced polymer composites, chiefly carbon fiber, reduces its weight by two-thirds while maintaining crashworthiness. Second, aerodynamic design and better tires reduce air resistance by as much as 70% and rolling resistance by up to 80%. Together, these innovations save about two-thirds of the fuel. Third, 30% to 50% of the remaining fuel is saved by using a "hybrid-electric" drive. In such a system, the wheels are turned by electric motors whose power is made onboard by a small engine or turbine, or even more efficiently by a fuel cell. The fuel cell generates electricity directly by chemically combining stored hydrogen with oxygen, producing pure hot water as its only by-product. Interactions between the small, clean, efficient power source and the ultralight, low-drag auto body then further reduce the weight, cost, and complexity of both. Fourth, much of the traditional hardware—from transmissions and differentials to gauges and certain parts of the suspension—can be replaced by electronics controlled with highly integrated, customizable, and upgradable software.

These technologies make it feasible to manufacture pollution-free, high-performance cars, sport utilities, pickup trucks, and vans that get 80 to 200 miles per gallon (or its energy equivalent in other fuels). These improvements will not require any compromise in quality or utility. Fuel savings will not come from making the vehicles small, sluggish, unsafe, or unaffordable, nor will they depend on government fuel taxes, mandates, or subsidies. Rather, Hypercars will succeed for the same reason that people buy compact discs instead of phonograph records: the CD is a superior product that redefines market expectations. From the manufacturers' perspective, Hypercars will cut cycle times, capital needs, body part counts, and assembly effort and space by as much as tenfold. Early adopters will have a huge competitive advantage—which is why dozens of corporations, including most automakers, are now racing to bring Hypercar-like products to market.[2]

In the long term, the Hypercar will transform industries other than automobiles. It will displace about an eighth of the steel market directly and most of the rest eventually, as carbon fiber becomes far cheaper. Hypercars and their cousins could ultimately save as much oil as OPEC now sells. Indeed, oil may well become uncompetitive as a fuel long before it becomes scarce and costly.

Similar challenges face the coal and electricity industries because the development of the Hypercar is likely to accelerate greatly the commercialization of inexpensive hydrogen fuel cells. These fuel cells will help shift power production from centralized coal-fired and nuclear power stations to networks of decentralized, small-scale generators. In fact, fuel-cell-powered Hypercars could themselves be part of these networks. They'd be, in effect, 20-kilowatt power plants on wheels. Given that cars are left parked—that is, unused—more than 95% of the time, these Hypercars could be plugged into a grid and could then sell back enough electricity to repay as much as half the predicted cost of leasing them. A national Hypercar fleet could ultimately have five to ten times the generating capacity of the national electric grid.

As radical as it sounds, the Hypercar is not an isolated case. Similar ideas are emerging in such industries as chemicals, semiconductors, general manufacturing, transportation, water and waste-water treatment, agriculture, forestry, energy, real estate, and urban design. For example, the amount of carbon dioxide released for each microchip manufactured can be reduced almost 100-fold through improvements that are now profitable or soon will be.

Some of the most striking developments come from emulating nature's techniques. In her book, *Biomimicry,* Janine Benyus points out that spiders convert digested crickets and flies into silk that's as strong as Kevlar without the need for boiling sulfuric acid and high-temperature extruders. Using no furnaces, abalone can convert seawater into an inner shell twice as tough as our best ceramics. Trees turn sunlight, water, soil, and air into cellulose, a sugar stronger than nylon but one-fourth as dense. They then bind it into wood, a natural composite with a higher bending strength than concrete, aluminum alloy, or steel. We may never become as skillful as spiders, abalone, or trees, but smart designers are already realizing that nature's environmentally benign chemistry offers attractive alternatives to industrial brute force.

Whether through better design or through new technologies, reducing waste represents a vast business opportunity. The U.S. economy is not even 10% as energy efficient as the laws of physics allow. Just the energy thrown off as waste heat by U.S. power stations equals the total energy use of Japan. Materials efficiency is even worse: only about 1% of all the materials mobilized to serve America is actually made into products and still in use six months after sale. In every sector, there are opportunities for reducing the amount of resources that go into a production process, the steps required to run that process, and the amount of pollution generated and by-products discarded at the end. These all represent avoidable costs and hence profits to be won.

Redesign Production According to Biological Models

In the second stage on the journey to natural capitalism, companies use closed-loop manufacturing to create new products and processes that can totally prevent waste. This plus more efficient production processes could cut companies' long-term materials requirements by more than 90% in most sectors.

The central principle of closed-loop manufacturing, as architect Paul Bierman-Lytle of the engineering firm CH2M Hill puts it, is "waste equals food." Every output of manufacturing should be either composted into natural nutrients or remanufactured into technical nutrients—that is, it should be returned to the ecosystem or recycled for further production. Closed-loop production systems are designed to eliminate any materials that incur disposal costs, especially toxic ones, because the alternative—isolating them to prevent harm to natural systems—tends to be costly and risky. Indeed, meeting EPA and OSHA standards by eliminating harmful materials often makes a manufacturing process cost less than the hazardous process it replaced. Motorola, for example, formerly used chlorofluorocarbons for cleaning printed circuit boards after soldering. When CFCs were outlawed because they destroy stratospheric ozone, Motorola at first explored such alternatives as orange-peel terpenes. But it turned out to be even cheaper—and to produce a better product—to redesign the whole soldering process so that it needed no cleaning operations or cleaning materials at all.

Closed-loop manufacturing is more than just a theory. The U.S. remanufacturing industry in 1996 reported revenues of $53 billion—more than consumer-durables manufacturing (appliances; furniture; audio, video, farm, and garden equipment). Xerox, whose bottom line has swelled by $700 million from remanufacturing, expects to save another $1 billion just by remanufacturing its new, entirely reusable or recyclable line of "green" photocopiers. What's more, policy makers in some countries are already taking steps to encourage industry to think along these lines. German law, for example, makes many manufacturers responsible for their products forever, and Japan is following suit.

Combining closed-loop manufacturing with resource efficiency is especially powerful. DuPont, for example, gets much of its polyester industrial film back from customers after they use it and recycles it into new film. DuPont also makes its polyester film ever stronger and thinner so it uses less material and costs less to make. Yet because the film performs better, customers are willing to pay more for it. As DuPont chairman Jack Krol noted in 1997, "Our ability to continually improve the inherent properties [of our films] enables this process [of developing more productive materials, at lower cost, and higher profits] to go on indefinitely."

Interface is leading the way to this next frontier of industrial ecology. While its competitors are "down cycling" nylon-and-PVC-based carpet into less valuable carpet backing, Interface has invented a new floor-covering material called Solenium, which can be completely remanufactured into identical new product. This fundamental innovation emerged from a clean-sheet redesign. Executives at Interface didn't ask how they could sell more carpet of the familiar kind; they asked how they could create a dream product that would best meet their customers' needs while protecting and nourishing natural capital.

Solenium lasts four times longer and uses 40% less material than ordinary carpets—an 86% reduction in materials intensity. What's more, Solenium is free of chlorine and other toxic materials, is virtually stainproof, doesn't grow mildew, can easily be cleaned with water, and offers aesthetic advantages over traditional carpets. It's so superior in every respect that Interface doesn't market it as an environmental product—just a better one.

Solenium is only one part of Interface's drive to eliminate every form of waste. Chairman Ray C. Anderson defines waste as "any measurable input that does not produce customer value," and he considers all inputs to be waste until shown otherwise. Between 1994 and 1998, this zero-waste approach led to a systematic treasure hunt that helped to keep resource inputs constant while revenues rose by $200 million. Indeed, $67 million of the revenue increase can be directly attributed to the company's 60% reduction in landfill waste.

Subsequently, president Charlie Eitel expanded the definition of waste to include all fossil fuel inputs, and now many customers are eager to buy products from the company's recently opened solar-powered carpet factory. Interface's green strategy has not only won plaudits from environmentalists, it has also proved a remarkably successful business strategy. Between 1993 and 1998, revenue has more than doubled, profits have more than tripled, and the number of employees has increased by 73%.

Change the Business Model

In addition to its drive to eliminate waste, Interface has made a fundamental shift in its business model—the third stage on the journey toward natural capitalism. The company has realized that clients want to walk on and look at carpets—but not necessarily to own them. Traditionally, broadloom carpets in office buildings are replaced every decade because some portions look worn out. When that happens, companies suffer the disruption of shutting down their offices and removing their furniture. Billions of pounds of carpets are removed each year and sent to landfills, where they will last up to 20,000 years. To escape this unproductive and wasteful cycle, Interface is transforming itself from a company that sells and fits carpets into one that provides floor-covering services.

Under its Evergreen Lease, Interface no longer sells carpets but rather leases a floor-covering service for a monthly fee, accepting responsibility for keeping the carpet fresh and clean. Monthly inspections detect and replace worn carpet tiles. Since at most 20% of an area typically shows at least 80% of the wear, replacing only the worn parts reduces the consumption of carpeting material by about 80%. It also minimizes the disruption that customers experience—worn tiles are seldom found under furniture. Finally, for the customer, leasing carpets can provide a tax advantage by turning a capital expenditure into a tax-deductible expense. The result: the customer gets cheaper and better services that cost the supplier far less to produce. Indeed, the energy saved from not producing a whole new carpet is in itself enough to produce all the carpeting that the new business model requires. Taken together, the 5-fold savings in carpeting material that Interface achieves through the Evergreen Lease and the 7-fold materials savings achieved through the use of Solenium deliver a stunning 35-fold reduction in the flow of materials needed to sustain a superior floor-covering service. Remanufacturing, and even making carpet initially from renewable materials, can then reduce the extraction of virgin resources essentially to the company's goal of zero.

Interface's shift to a service-leasing business reflects a fundamental change from the basic model of most manufacturing companies, which still look on their businesses as machines for producing and selling products. The more products sold, the better—at least for the company, if not always for the customer or the earth. But any model that wastes natural resources also wastes money. Ultimately, that model will be unable to compete with a service model that emphasizes solving problems and building long-term relationships with customers rather than making and selling products. The shift to what James Womack of the Lean Enterprise Institute calls a "solutions economy" will almost always improve customer value *and* providers' bottom lines because it aligns both parties' interests, offering rewards for doing more and better with less.

Interface is not alone. Elevator giant Schindler, for example, prefers leasing vertical transportation services to selling elevators because leasing lets it capture the savings from its elevators' lower energy and maintenance costs. Dow Chemical and Safety-Kleen prefer leasing dissolving services to selling solvents because they can reuse the same solvent scores of times, reducing costs. United Technologies' Carrier division, the world's largest manufacturer of air conditioners, is shifting its mission from selling air conditioners to leasing comfort. Making its air conditioners more durable and efficient may compromise future equipment sales, but it provides what customers want and will pay for—better comfort at lower cost. But Carrier is going even further. It's starting to team up with other companies to make buildings more efficient so that they need less air-conditioning, or even none at all, to yield the same level of comfort. Carrier will get paid to provide the agreed-upon level of comfort, however that's delivered. Higher profits will come from providing better solutions rather than from selling more equipment. Since comfort with little or no air-conditioning (via better building design) works better and costs less than comfort with copious air-conditioning, Carrier is smart to capture this opportunity itself before its competitors do. As they say at 3M: "We'd rather eat our *own* lunch, thank you."

The shift to a service business model promises benefits not just to participating businesses but to the entire economy as well. Womack points out that by helping customers reduce their need for capital goods such as carpets or elevators, and by rewarding suppliers for extending and maximizing asset values rather than for churning them, adoption of the service model will reduce the volatility in the turnover of capital goods that lies at the heart of the business cycle. That would significantly reduce the overall volatility of the world's economy. At present, the producers of capital goods face feast or famine because the buying decisions of households and corporations are extremely sensitive to fluctuating income. But in a continuous-flow-of-services economy, those swings would be greatly reduced, bringing a welcome stability to businesses. Excess capacity—another form of waste and source of risk—need no longer be retained for meeting peak demand. The result of adopting the new model would be an economy in which we grow and get richer by using less and become stronger by being leaner and more stable.

Reinvest in Natural Capital

The foundation of textbook capitalism is the prudent reinvestment of earnings in productive capital. Natural capitalists who have dramatically raised their resource productivity, closed their loops, and shifted to a solutions-based business model have one key task remaining. They must reinvest in restoring, sustaining, and expanding the most important form of capital—their own natural habitat and biological resource base.

This was not always so important. Until recently, business could ignore damage to the ecosystem because it didn't affect production and didn't increase costs. But that situation is changing. In 1998 alone, violent weather displaced 300 million people and caused upwards of $90 billion worth of damage, representing more weather-related destruction than was reported through the entire decade of the 1980s. The increase in damage is strongly linked to deforestation and climate change, factors that accelerate the frequency and severity of natural disasters and are the consequences of inefficient industrialization. If the flow of services from industrial systems is to be sustained or increased in the future for a growing population, the vital flow of services from living systems will have to be maintained or increased as well. Without reinvestment in natural capital, shortages of ecosystem services are likely to become the limiting factor to prosperity in the next century. When a manufacturer realizes that a supplier of key components is overextended and running behind on deliveries, it takes immediate action lest its own production lines come to a halt. The ecosystem is a supplier of key components for the life of the planet, and it is now falling behind on its orders.

Failure to protect and reinvest in natural capital can also hit a company's revenues indirectly. Many companies are discovering that public perceptions of environmental responsibility, or its lack thereof, affect sales. MacMillan Bloedel, targeted by environmental activists as an emblematic clear-cutter and chlorine user, lost 5% of its sales almost overnight when dropped as a U.K. supplier by Scott Paper and Kimberly-Clark. Numerous case studies show that companies leading the way in implementing changes that help protect the environment tend to gain disproportionate advantage, while companies perceived as irresponsible lose their franchise, their legitimacy, and their shirts. Even businesses that claim to be committed to the concept of sustainable development but whose strategy is seen as mistaken, like Monsanto, are encountering stiffening public resistance to their products. Not surprisingly, University of Oregon business professor Michael Russo, along with many other analysts, has found that a strong environmental rating is "a consistent predictor of profitability."

The pioneering corporations that have made reinvestments in natural capital are starting to see some interesting paybacks. The independent power producer AES, for example, has long pursued a policy of planting trees to offset the carbon emissions of its power plants. That ethical stance, once thought quixotic, now looks like a smart investment because a dozen brokers are now starting to create markets in carbon reduction. Similarly, certification by the Forest Stewardship Council of certain sustainably grown and harvested products has given Collins Pine the extra profit margins that enabled its U.S. manufacturing operations to survive brutal competition. Taking an even longer view, Swiss Re and other European reinsurers are seeking to cut their storm-damage losses by pressing for international public policy to protect the climate and by investing in climate-safe technologies that also promise good profits. Yet most companies still do not realize that a vibrant ecological web underpins their survival and their business success. Enriching natural capital is not just a public good—it is vital to every company's longevity.

It turns out that changing industrial processes so that they actually replenish and magnify the stock of natural capital can prove especially profitable because nature does the production; people need just step back and let life flourish. Industries that directly harvest living resources, such as forestry, farming, and fishing, offer the most suggestive examples. Here are three:

- Allan Savory of the Center for Holistic Management in Albuquerque, New Mexico, has redesigned cattle ranching to raise the carrying capacity of rangelands, which have often been degraded not by overgrazing but by undergrazing and grazing the wrong way. Savory's solution is to keep the cattle moving from place to place, grazing intensively but briefly at each site, so that they mimic the dense but constantly moving herds of native grazing animals that coevolved with grasslands. Thousands of ranchers are estimated to be applying this approach, improving both their range and their profits. This "management-intensive rotational grazing" method, long standard in New Zealand, yields such clearly superior returns that over 15% of Wisconsin's dairy farms have adopted it in the past few years.

- The California Rice Industry Association has discovered that letting nature's diversity flourish can be more profitable than forcing it to produce a single product. By flooding 150,000 to 200,000 acres of Sacramento valley rice fields—about 30% of California's rice-growing area—after harvest, farmers are able to create seasonal wetlands that support millions of wildfowl, replenish groundwater, improve fertility, and yield other valuable benefits. In addition, the farmers bale and sell the rice straw, whose high silica content—formerly an air-pollution hazard when the straw was burned—adds insect resistance and hence value as a construction material when it's resold instead.

- John Todd of Living Technologies in Burlington, Vermont, has used biological Living Machines—linked tanks of bacteria, algae, plants, and other organisms—to turn sewage into clean water. That not only yields cleaner water at a reduced cost, with no toxicity or odor, but it also produces commercially valuable flowers and makes the plant compatible with its residential neighborhood. A similar plant at the Ethel M Chocolates factory in Las Vegas, Nevada, not only handles difficult industrial wastes effectively but is showcased in its public tours.

Although such practices are still evolving, the broad lessons they teach are clear. In almost all climates, soils, and societies, working with nature is more productive than working against it. Reinvesting in nature allows farmers, fishermen, and forest managers to match or exceed the high yields and profits sustained by traditional input-intensive, chemically driven practices. Although much of mainstream business is still headed the other way, the profitability of sustainable, nature-emulating practices is already being proven. In the future, many industries that don't now consider themselves dependent on a biological resource base will become more so as they shift their raw materials and production processes more to biological ones. There is evidence that many business leaders are starting to think this way. The consulting firm Arthur D. Little surveyed a group of North American and European business leaders and found that 83% of them already believe that they can derive "real business value [from implementing a] sustainable-development approach to strategy and operations."

A Broken Compass?

If the road ahead is this clear, why are so many companies straying or falling by the wayside? We believe the reason is that the instruments companies use to set their targets, measure their performance, and hand out rewards are faulty. In other words, the markets are full of distortions and perverse incentives. Of the more than 60 specific forms of misdirection that we have identified,[3] the most obvious involve the ways companies allocate capital and the way governments set policy and impose taxes. Merely correcting these defective practices would uncover huge opportunities for profit.

Consider how companies make purchasing decisions. Decisions to buy small items are typically based on their initial cost rather than their full life-cycle cost, a practice that can add up to major wastage. Distribution transformers that supply electricity to buildings and factories, for example, are a minor item at just $320 apiece, and most companies try to save a quick buck by buying the lowest-price models. Yet nearly all the nation's electricity must flow through transformers, and using the cheaper but less efficient models wastes $1 billion a year. Such examples are legion. Equipping standard new office-lighting circuits with fatter wire that reduces electrical resistance could generate after-tax returns of 193% a year. Instead, wire as thin as the National Electrical Code permits is usually selected because it costs less up-front. But the code is meant only to prevent fires from overheated wiring, not to save money. Ironically, an electrician who chooses fatter wire—thereby reducing long-term electricity bills—doesn't get the job. After paying for the extra copper, he's no longer the low bidder.

Some companies do consider more than just the initial price in their purchasing decisions but still don't go far enough. Most of them use a crude payback estimate rather than more accurate metrics like discounted cash flow. A few years ago, the median simple payback these companies were demanding from energy efficiency was 1.9 years. That's equivalent to requiring an after-tax return of around 71% per year—about six times the marginal cost of capital.

Most companies also miss major opportunities by treating their facilities costs as an overhead to be minimized, typically by laying off engineers, rather than as profit center to be optimized—by using those engineers to save resources. Deficient measurement and accounting practices also prevent companies from allocating costs—and waste—with any accuracy. For example, only a few semiconductor plants worldwide regularly and accurately measure how much energy they're using to produce a unit of chilled water or clean air for their clean-room production facilities. That makes it hard for them to improve efficiency. In fact, in an effort to save time, semiconductor makers frequently build new plants as exact copies of previous ones—a design method nicknamed "infectious repetitis."

Many executives pay too little attention to saving resources because they are often a small percentage of total costs (energy costs run to about 2% in most industries). But those resource savings drop straight to the bottom line and so represent a far greater percentage of profits. Many executives also think they already "did" efficiency in the 1970s, when the oil shock forced them to rethink old habits. They're forgetting that with today's far better technologies, it's profitable to start all over again. Malden Mills, the Massachusetts maker of such products as Polartec, was already using "efficient" metal-halide lamps in the mid-1990s. But a recent warehouse retrofit reduced the energy used for lighting by another 93%, improved visibility, and paid for itself in 18 months.

The way people are rewarded often creates perverse incentives. Architects and engineers, for example, are traditionally compensated for what they spend, not for what they save. Even the striking economics of the retrofit design for the Chicago office tower described earlier wasn't incentive enough actually to implement it. The property was controlled by a leasing agent who earned a commission every time she leased space, so she didn't want to wait the few extra months needed to refit the building. Her decision to reject the efficiency-quadrupling renovation proved costly for both her and her client. The building was so uncomfortable and expensive to occupy that it didn't lease, so ultimately the owner had to unload it at a firesale price. Moreover, the new owner will for the next 20 years be deprived of the opportunity to save capital cost.

If corporate practices obscure the benefits of natural capitalism, government policy positively undermines it. In nearly every country on the planet, tax laws penalize what we want more of—jobs and income—while subsidizing what we want less of—resource depletion and pollution. In every state but Oregon, regulated utilities are rewarded for selling more energy, water, and other resources, and penalized for selling less, even if increased production would cost more than improved customer efficiency. In most of America's arid western states, use-it-or-lose-it water laws encourage inefficient water consumption. Additionally, in many towns, inefficient use of land is enforced through outdated regulations, such as guidelines for ultrawide suburban streets recommended by 1950s civil-defense planners to accommodate the heavy equipment needed to clear up rubble after a nuclear attack.

The costs of these perverse incentives are staggering: $300 billion in annual energy wasted in the United States, and $1 trillion already misallocated to unnecessary air-conditioning equipment and the power supplies to run it (about 40% of the nation's peak electric load). Across the entire economy, unneeded expenditures to subsidize, encourage, and try to remedy inefficiency and damage that should not have occurred in the first place probably account for most, if not all, of the GDP growth of the past two decades. Indeed, according to former World Bank economist Herman Daly and his colleague John Cobb (along with many other analysts), Americans are hardly better off than they were in 1980. But if the U.S. government and private industry could redirect the dollars currently earmarked for remedial costs toward reinvestment in natural and human capital, they could bring about a genuine improvement in the nation's welfare. Companies, too, are finding that wasting resources also means wasting money and people. These intertwined forms of waste have equally intertwined solutions. Firing the unproductive tons, gallons, and kilowatt-hours often makes it possible to keep the people, who will have more and better work to do.

Recognizing the Scarcity Shift

In the end, the real trouble with our economic compass is that it points in exactly the wrong direction. Most businesses are behaving as if people were still scarce and nature still abundant—the conditions that helped to fuel the first Industrial Revolution. At that time, people were relatively scarce compared with the present-day population. The rapid mechanization of the textile industries caused explosive economic growth that created labor shortages in the factory and the field. The Industrial Revolution, responding to those shortages and mechanizing one industry after another, made people a hundred times more productive than they had ever been.

The logic of economizing on the scarcest resource, because it limits progress, remains correct. But the pattern of scarcity is shifting: now people aren't scarce but nature is. This shows up first in industries that depend directly on ecological health. Here, production is increasingly constrained by fish rather than by boats and nets, by forests rather than by chain saws, by fertile topsoil rather than by plows. Moreover, unlike the traditional factors of industrial production—capital and labor—the biological limiting factors cannot be substituted for one another. In the industrial system, we can easily exchange machinery for labor. But no technology or amount of money can substitute for a stable climate and a productive biosphere. Even proper pricing can't replace the priceless.

Natural capitalism addresses those problems by reintegrating ecological with economic goals. Because it is both necessary and profitable, it will subsume traditional industrialism within a new economy and a new paradigm of production, just as industrialism previously subsumed agrarianism. The companies that first make the changes we have described will have a competitive edge. Those that don't make that effort won't be a problem because ultimately they won't be around. In making that choice, as Henry Ford said, "Whether you believe you can, or whether you believe you can't, you're absolutely right."

Notes

1. Our book, *Natural Capitalism,* provides hundreds of examples of how companies of almost every type and size, often through modest shifts in business logic and practice, have dramatically improved their bottom lines.
2. Nonproprietary details are posted at http://www.hypercar.com.
3. Summarized in the report "Climate: Making Sense *and* Making Money" at http://www.rmi.org/catalog/climate.htm.

Originally published in May–June 1999
Reprint 99309

Beyond Greening: Strategies for a Sustainable World

STUART L. HART

Executive Summary

THREE DECADES into the environmental revolution, many companies in the industrialized nations have recognized that they can reduce pollution and increase profits at the same time. But beyond corporate "greening" lies the enormous challenge–and opportunity–to develop a sustainable global economy, one that the planet is capable of supporting indefinitely.

Stuart Hart, director of the Corporate Environmental Management Program at the University of Michigan School of Business, explains the imperative of sustainable development and provides a framework for identifying the business opportunities behind sustainability. The dangers today are clear: exploding population growth, rapid depletion of resources, and ever more industrialization and urbanization are creating a terrible environmental burden.

Companies normally frame greening in terms of risk reduction, reengineering, or cost cutting. But, says Hart, when greening becomes part of strategy, opportunities of potentially staggering proportions open up. A number of companies are moving in that direction. BASF, for example, is colocating plants to make the recycling of waste feasible, and Xerox is reusing parts from leased copiers on new machines.

Hart identifies three stages of environmental strategy: pollution prevention, product stewardship, and the development of clean technology. But companies will not benefit from such efforts unless they draw a road map that can show them how new products and services must evolve and what competencies they will need. Businesses that create a vision of sustainability will be ready to take advantage of the opportunities presented by the need for a sustainable global economy.

THE ENVIRONMENTAL REVOLUTION has been almost three decades in the making, and it has changed forever how companies do business. In the 1960s and 1970s, corporations were in a state of denial regarding their impact on the environment. Then a series of highly visible ecological problems created a groundswell of support for strict government regulation. In the United States, Lake Erie was dead. In Europe, the Rhine was on fire. In Japan, people were dying of mercury poisoning.

Today many companies have accepted their responsibility to do no harm to the environment. Products and production processes are becoming cleaner; and where such change is under way, the environment is on the mend. In the industrialized nations, more and more companies are "going green" as they realize that they can reduce pollution and increase profits simultaneously. We have come a long way.

But the distance we've traveled will seem small when, in 30 years, we look back at the 1990s. Beyond greening lies an enormous challenge—and an enormous opportunity. The challenge is to develop a *sustainable global economy:* an economy that the planet is capable of supporting indefinitely. Although we may be approaching ecological recovery in the developed world, the planet as a whole remains on an unsustainable course. Those who think that sustainability is only a matter of pollution control are missing the bigger picture. Even if all the companies in the developed world were to achieve zero emissions by the year 2000, the earth would still be stressed beyond what biologists refer to as its carrying capacity. Increasingly, the scourges of the late twentieth century—depleted farmland, fisheries, and forests; choking urban pollution; poverty; infectious disease; and migration—are spilling over geopolitical borders. The simple fact is this: in meeting our needs, we are destroying the ability of future generations to meet theirs.

The roots of the problem—explosive population growth and rapid economic development in the emerging economies—are political and social issues that exceed the mandate and the capabilities of any corporation. At the same time, corporations are the only organizations with the resources, the technology, the global reach, and, ultimately, the motivation to achieve sustainability.

It is easy to state the case in the negative: faced with impoverished customers, degraded environments, failing political systems, and unraveling societies, it will be increasingly difficult for corporations to do business. But the positive case is even more powerful. The more we learn about the challenges of sustainability, the clearer it is that we are poised at the threshold of a historic moment in which many of the world's industries may be transformed.

To date, the business logic for greening has been largely operational or technical: bottom-up pollution-prevention programs have saved companies billions of dollars. However, few executives realize that environmental opportunities might actually become a major source of *revenue growth.* Greening has been framed in terms of risk reduction, reengineering, or cost cutting. Rarely is greening linked to strategy or technology development, and as a result, most companies fail to recognize opportunities of potentially staggering proportions.

Worlds in Collision

The achievement of sustainability will mean billions of dollars in products, services, and technologies that barely exist today. Whereas yesterday's businesses were often oblivious to their negative impact on the environment and today's responsible businesses strive for zero impact, tomorrow's businesses must learn to make a positive impact. Increasingly, companies will be selling solutions to the world's environmental problems.

Envisioning tomorrow's businesses, therefore, requires a clear understanding of those problems. To move beyond greening to sustainability, we must first unravel a complex set of global interdependencies. In fact, the global economy is really three different, overlapping economies.

The *market economy* is the familiar world of commerce comprising both the developed nations and the emerging economies.[1] About a billion people—one-sixth of the world's population—live in the developed countries of the market economy. Those affluent societies account for more than 75% of the world's energy and resource consumption and create the bulk of industrial, toxic, and consumer waste. The developed economies thus leave large ecological *footprints*—defined as the amount of land required to meet a typical consumer's needs.

Despite such intense use of energy and materials, however, levels of pollution are relatively low in the developed economies. Three factors account for this seeming paradox: stringent environmental regulations, the greening of industry, and the relocation of the most polluting activities (such as commodity processing and heavy manufacturing) to the emerging market economies. Thus to some extent the greening of the developed world has been at the expense of the environments in emerging economies. Given the much larger population base in those countries, their rapid industrialization could easily offset the environmental gains made in the developed economies. Consider, for example, that the emerging economies in Asia and Latin America (and now Eastern Europe and the former Soviet Union) have added nearly 2 billion people to the market economy over the past 40 years.

With economic growth comes urbanization. Today one of every three people in the world lives in a city. By 2025, it will be two out of three. Demographers predict that by that year there will be well over 30 megacities with populations exceeding 8 million and more than 500 cities with populations exceeding 1 million. Urbanization on this scale presents enormous infrastructural and environmental challenges.

Because industrialization has focused initially on commodities and heavy manufacturing, cities in many emerging economies suffer from oppressive levels of pollution. Acid rain is a growing problem, especially in places where coal combustion is unregulated. The World Bank estimates that by 2010 there will be more than 1 billion motor vehicles in the world. Concentrated in cities, they will double current levels of energy use, smog precursors, and emissions of greenhouse gas.

The second economy is the *survival economy:* the traditional, village-based way of life found in the rural parts of most developing countries. It is made up of 3 billion people, mainly Africans, Indians, and Chinese who are subsistence oriented and meet their basic needs directly from nature. Demographers generally agree that the world's population, currently growing by about 90 million people per year, will roughly double over the next 40 years. The developing nations will account for 90% of that growth, and most of it will occur in the survival economy.

Owing in part to the rapid expansion of the market economy, existence in the survival economy is becoming increasingly precarious. Extractive industries and infrastructure development have, in many cases, degraded the ecosystems upon which the survival economy depends. Rural populations are driven further into poverty as they compete for scarce natural resources. Women and children now spend on average four to six hours per day searching for fuelwood and four to six hours per week drawing and carrying water. Ironically, those conditions encourage high fertility rates because, in the short run, children help the family to garner needed resources. But in the long run, population growth in the survival economy only reinforces a vicious cycle of resource depletion and poverty.

Short-term survival pressures often force these rapidly growing rural populations into practices that cause long-term damage to forests, soil, and water. When wood becomes scarce, people burn dung for fuel, one of the greatest—and least well-known—environmental hazards in the world today. Contaminated drinking water is an equally grave problem. The World Health Organization estimates that burning dung and drinking contaminated water together cause 8 million deaths per year.

As it becomes more and more difficult to live off the land, millions of desperate people migrate to already overcrowded cities. In China, for example, an estimated 120 million people now roam from city to city, landless and jobless, driven from their villages by deforestation, soil erosion, floods, or droughts. Worldwide, the number of such "environmental refugees" from the survival economy may be as high as 500 million people, and the figure is growing.

The third economy is *nature's economy,* which consists of the natural systems and resources that support the market and the survival economies. Nonrenewable resources, such as oil, metals, and other minerals, are finite. Renewable resources, such as soils and forests, will replenish themselves—as long as their use does not exceed critical thresholds.

Technological innovations have created substitutes for many commonly used nonrenewable resources; for example, optical fiber now replaces copper wire. And in the developed economies, demand for some virgin materials may actually diminish in the decades ahead because of reuse and recycling. Ironically, the greatest threat to sustainable development today is depletion of the world's *renewable* resources.

Forests, soils, water, and fisheries are all being pushed beyond their limits by human population growth and rapid industrial development. Insufficient fresh water may prove to be the most vexing problem in the developing world over the next decade, as agricultural, commercial, and residential uses increase. Water tables are being drawn down at an alarming rate, especially in the most heavily populated nations, such as China and India.

Soil is another resource at risk. More than 10% of the world's topsoil has been seriously eroded. Available cropland and rangeland are shrinking. Existing crop varieties are no longer responding to increased use of fertilizer. As a consequence, per capita world production of both grain and meat peaked and began to decline during the 1980s. Meanwhile, the world's 18 major oceanic fisheries have now reached or actually exceeded their maximum sustainable yields.

By some estimates, humankind now uses more than 40% of the planet's net primary productivity. If, as projected, the population doubles over the next 40 years, we may outcompete most other animal species for food, driving many to extinction. In short, human activity now exceeds sustainability on a global scale. (See the exhibit "Major Challenges to Sustainability.")

As we approach the twenty-first century, the interdependence of the three economic spheres is increasingly evident. In fact, the three economies have become worlds in collision, creating the major social and environmental challenges facing the planet: climate change, pollution, resource depletion, poverty, and inequality.

Major Challenges to Sustainability

	Pollution	**Depletion**	**Poverty**
Developed economies	• greenhouse gases • use of toxic materials • contaminated sites	• scarcity of materials • insufficient reuse and recycling	• urban and minority unemployment
Emerging economies	• industrial emissions • contaminated water • lack of sewage treatment	• overexploitation of renewable resources • overuse of water for irrigation	• migration to cities • lack of skilled workers • income inequality
Survival economies	• dung and wood burning • lack of sanitation • ecosystem destruction due to development	• deforestation • overgrazing • soil loss	• population growth • low status of women • dislocation

Consider, for example, that the average American today consumes 17 times more than his or her Mexican counterpart (emerging economy) and hundreds of times more than the average Ethiopian (survival economy). The levels of material and energy consumption in the United States require large quantities of raw materials and commodities, sourced increasingly from the survival economy and produced in emerging economies.

In the survival economy, massive infrastructure development (for example, dams, irrigation projects, highways, mining operations, and power generation projects), often aided by agencies, banks, and corporations in the developed countries, has provided access to raw materials. Unfortunately, such development has often had devastating consequences for nature's economy and has tended to strengthen existing political and economic elites, with little benefit to those in the survival economy.

At the same time, infrastructure development projects have contributed to a global glut of raw materials and hence to a long-term fall in commodity prices. And as commodity prices have fallen relative to the prices of manufactured goods, the currencies of developing countries have weakened and their terms of trade have become less favorable. Their purchasing power declines while their already substantial debt load becomes even larger. The net effect of this dynamic has been the transfer of vast amounts of wealth (estimated at $40 billion per year since 1985) from developing to developed countries, producing a vicious cycle of resource exploitation and pollution to service mounting debt. Today developing nations have a combined debt of more than $1.2 trillion, equal to nearly half of their collective gross national product.

Strategies for a Sustainable World

Nearly three decades ago, environmentalists such as Paul Ehrlich and Barry Commoner made this simple but powerful observation about sustainable development: the total environmental burden (EB) created by human activity is a function of three factors. They are population (P); affluence (A), which is a proxy for consumption; and technology (T), which is how wealth is created. The product of these three factors determines the total environmental burden. It can be expressed as a formula: $EB = P \times A \times T$.

Achieving sustainability will require stabilizing or reducing the environmental burden. That can be done by decreasing the human population, lowering the level of affluence (consumption), or changing fundamentally the technology used to create wealth. The first option, lowering the human population, does not appear feasible short of draconian political measures or the occurrence of a major public-health crisis that causes mass mortality.

The second option, decreasing the level of affluence, would only make the problem worse, because poverty and population growth go hand in hand: demographers have long known that birth rates are inversely correlated with level of education and standard of living. Thus stabilizing the human population will require improving the education and economic standing of the world's poor, particularly women of childbearing age. That can be accomplished only by creating wealth on a massive scale. Indeed, it may be necessary to grow the world economy as much as tenfold just to provide basic amenities to a population of 8 billion to 10 billion.

That leaves the third option: changing the technology used to create the goods and services that constitute the world's wealth. Although population and consumption may be societal issues, technology is the business of business.

If economic activity must increase tenfold over what it is today just to provide the bare essentials to a population double its current size, then technology will have to improve twentyfold merely to keep the planet at its current levels of environmental burden. Those who believe that ecological disaster will somehow be averted must also appreciate the commercial implications of such a belief: over the next decade or so, sustainable development will constitute one of the biggest opportunities in the history of commerce.

Nevertheless, as of today few companies have incorporated sustainability into their strategic thinking. Instead, environmental strategy consists largely of piecemeal projects aimed at controlling or preventing pollution. Focusing on sustainability requires putting business strategies to a new test. Taking the entire planet as the context in which they do business, companies must ask whether they are part of the solution to social and environmental problems or part of the problem. Only when a company thinks in those terms can it begin to develop a vision of sustainability—a shaping logic that goes beyond today's internal, operational focus on greening to a more external, strategic focus on sustainable development. Such a vision is needed to guide companies through three stages of environmental strategy.

Stage one: Pollution prevention. The first step for most companies is to make the shift from pollution control to pollution prevention. Pollution control means cleaning up waste after it has been created. Pollution prevention focuses on minimizing or eliminating waste before it is created. Much like total quality management, pollution prevention strategies depend on continuous improvement efforts to reduce waste and energy use. This transformation is driven by a compelling logic: pollution prevention pays. Emerging global standards for environmental management systems (ISO 14,000, for example) also have created strong incentives for companies to develop such capabilities.

Over the past decade, companies have sought to avoid colliding with nature's economy (and incurring the associated added costs) through greening and prevention strategies. Aeroquip Corporation, a $2.5 billion manufacturer of hoses, fittings, and couplings, saw an opportunity here. Like most industrial suppliers, Aeroquip never thought of itself as a provider of environmental solutions. But in 1990, its executives realized that the company's products might be especially valuable in meeting the need to reduce waste and prevent pollution. Aeroquip has generated a $250 million business by focusing its attention on developing products that reduce emissions. As companies in emerging economies realize the competitive benefits of using raw materials and resources more productively, businesses like Aeroquip's will continue to grow.

The emerging economies cannot afford to repeat all the environmental mistakes of Western development. With the sustainability imperative in mind, BASF, the German chemical giant, is helping to design and build chemical industries in China, India, Indonesia, and Malaysia that are less polluting than in the past. By colocating facilities that in the West have been geographically dispersed, BASF is able to create industrial ecosystems in which the waste from one process becomes the raw material for another. Colocation solves a problem common in the West, where recycling waste is often infeasible because transporting it from one site to another is dangerous and costly.

Stage two: Product stewardship. Product stewardship focuses on minimizing not only pollution from manufacturing but also all environmental impacts associated with the full life cycle of a product. As companies in stage one move closer to zero emissions, reducing the use of materials and production of waste requires fundamental changes in underlying product and process design.

Design for environment (DFE), a tool for creating products that are easier to recover, reuse, or recycle, is becoming increasingly important. With DFE, all the effects that a product could have on the environment are examined during its design phase. Cradle-to-grave analysis begins and ends outside the boundaries of a company's operations—it includes a full assessment of all inputs to the product and examines how customers use and dispose of it. DFE thus captures a broad range of external perspectives by including technical staff, environmental experts, end customers, and even community representatives in the process. Dow Chemical Company has pioneered the use of a board-level advisory panel of environmental experts and external representatives to aid its product-stewardship efforts.

By reducing materials and energy consumption, DFE can be highly profitable. Consider Xerox Corporation's Asset Recycle Management (ARM) program, which uses leased Xerox copiers as sources of high-quality, low-cost parts and components for new machines. A well-developed infrastructure for taking back leased copiers combined with a sophisticated remanufacturing process allows parts and components to be reconditioned, tested, and then reassembled into "new" machines. Xerox estimates that ARM savings in raw materials, labor, and waste disposal in 1995 alone were in the $300-million to $400-million range. In taking recycling to this level, Xerox has reconceptualized its business. By redefining the product-in-use as part of the company's asset base, Xerox has discovered a way to add value and lower costs. It can continually provide its lease customers with the latest product upgrades, giving them state-of-the-art functionality with minimal environmental impact.

Product stewardship is thus one way to reduce consumption in the developed economies. It may also aid the quest for sustainability because developing nations often try to emulate what they see happening in the developed nations. Properly executed, product stewardship also offers the potential for revenue growth through product differentiation. For example, Dunlop Tire Corporation and Akzo Nobel recently announced a new radial tire that makes use of an aramid fiber belt rather than the conventional steel belt. The new design makes recycling easier because it eliminates the expensive cryogenic crushing required to separate the steel belts from the tire's other materials. Because the new fiber-belt tire is 30% lighter, it dramatically improves gas mileage. Moreover, it is a safer tire because it improves the traction control of antilock braking systems.

The evolution from pollution prevention to product stewardship is now happening in multinational companies such as Dow, DuPont, Monsanto, Xerox, ABB, Philips, and Sony. For example, as part of a larger sustainability strategy dubbed A Growing Partnership with Nature, DuPont's agricultural-products business developed a new type of herbicide that has helped farmers around the world reduce their annual use of chemicals by more than 45 million pounds. The new Sulfonylurea herbicides have also led to a 1-billion-pound reduction in the amount of chemical waste produced in the manufacture of agricultural chemicals. These herbicides are effective at 1% to 5% of the application rates of traditional chemicals, are nontoxic to animals and nontarget species, and biodegrade in the soil, leaving virtually no residue on crops. Because they require so much less material in their manufacture, they are also highly profitable.

Stage three: Clean technology. Companies with their eye on the future can begin to plan for and invest in tomorrow's technologies. The simple fact is that the existing technology base in many industries is not environmentally sustainable. The chemical industry, for example, while having made substantial headway over the past decade in pollution prevention and product stewardship, is still limited by its dependence on the chlorine molecule. (Many organochlorides are toxic or persistent or bioaccumulative.) As long as the industry relies on its historical competencies in chlorine chemistry, it will have trouble making major progress toward sustainability.

Monsanto is one company that is consciously developing new competencies. It is shifting the technology base for its agriculture business from bulk chemicals to biotechnology. It is betting that the bioengineering of crops rather than the application of chemical pesticides or fertilizers represents a sustainable path to increased agricultural yields. (See "Growth Through Global Sustainability: An Interview with Monsanto's CEO, Robert B. Shapiro," by Joan Magretta, in HBR January-February 1997.)

Clean technologies are desperately needed in the emerging economies of Asia. Urban pollution there has reached oppressive levels. But precisely because manufacturing growth is so high—capital stock doubles every six years—there is an unprecedented opportunity to replace current product and process technologies with new, cleaner ones.

Japan's Research Institute for Innovative Technology for the Earth is one of several new research and technology consortia focusing on the development and commercialization of clean technologies for the developing world. Having been provided with funding and staff by the Japanese government and more than 40 corporations, RITE has set forth an ambitious 100-year plan to create the next generation of power technology, which will eliminate or neutralize greenhouse gas emissions.

Sustainability Vision

Pollution prevention, product stewardship, and clean technology all move a company toward sustainability. But without a framework to give direction to those activities, their impact will dissipate. A vision of sustainability for an industry or a company is like a road map to the future, showing the way products and services must evolve and what new competencies will be needed to get there. Few companies today have such a road map. Ironically, chemical companies, regarded only a decade ago as the worst environmental villains, are among the few large corporations to have engaged the challenge of sustainable development seriously.

Companies can begin by taking stock of each component of what I call their *sustainability portfolio.* (See the exhibit "The Sustainability Portfolio.") Is there an

The Sustainability Portfolio

This simple diagnostic tool can help any company determine whether its strategy is consistent with sustainability. First, assess your company's capability in each of the four quadrants by answering the questions in each box. Then rate yourself on the following scale for each quadrant: 1–nonexistent; 2–emerging; 3–established; or 4–institutionalized.

Most companies will be heavily skewed toward the lower left-hand quadrant, reflecting investment in pollution prevention. However, without investments in future technologies and markets (the upper half of the portfolio), the company's environmental strategy will not meet evolving needs.

Unbalanced portfolios spell trouble; a bottom-heavy portfolio suggests a good position today but future vulnerability. A top-heavy portfolio indicates a vision of sustainability without the operational or analytical skills needed to implement it. A portfolio skewed to the left side of the chart indicates a preoccupation with handling the environmental challenge through internal process improvements and technology-development initiatives. Finally, a portfolio skewed to the right side, although highly open and public, runs the risk of being labeled a "greenwash" because the underlying plant operations and core technology still cause significant environmental harm.

	Internal	External
Tomorrow	**Clean technology** Is the environmental performance of our products limited by our existing competency base? Is there potential to realize major improvements through new technology?	**Sustainability vision** Does our corporate vision direct us toward the solution of social and environmental problems? Does our vision guide the development of new technologies, markets, products, and processes?
Today	**Pollution prevention** Where are the most significant waste and emission streams from our current operations? Can we lower costs and risks by eliminating waste at the source or by using it as useful input?	**Product stewardship** What are the implications for product design and development if we assume responsibility for a product's entire life cycle? Can we add value or lower costs while simultaneously reducing the impact of our products?

overarching vision of sustainability that gives direction to the company's activities? To what extent has the company progressed through the three stages of environmental strategy—from pollution prevention to product stewardship to clean technology?

Consider the auto industry. During the 1970s, government regulation of tailpipe emissions forced the industry to focus on pollution control. In the 1980s, the industry began to tackle pollution prevention. Initiatives such as the Corporate Average Fuel Efficiency requirement and the Toxic Release Inventory led auto companies to examine their product designs and manufacturing processes in order to improve fuel economy and lower emissions from their plants.

The 1990s are witnessing the first signs of product stewardship. In Germany, the 1990 "take-back" law required auto manufacturers to take responsibility for their vehicles at the end of their useful lives. Innovators such as BMW have influenced the design of new cars with their *design for disassembly* efforts. Industry-level consortia such as the Partnership for a New Generation of Vehicles are driven largely by the product stewardship logic of lowering the environmental impact of automobiles throughout their life cycle.

Early attempts to promote clean technology include such initiatives as California's zero-emission vehicle law and the U.N. Climate Change Convention, which ultimately will limit greenhouse gases on a global scale. But early efforts by industry incumbents have been either incremental—for example, natural-gas vehicles—or defensive in nature. Electric-vehicle programs, for instance, have been used to demonstrate the infeasibility of this technology rather than to lead the industry to a fundamentally cleaner technology.

Although the auto industry has made progress, it falls far short of sustainability. For the vast majority of auto companies, pollution prevention and product stewardship are the end of the road. Most auto executives assume that if they close the loop in both production and design, they will have accomplished all the necessary environmental objectives.

But step back and try to imagine a sustainable vision for the industry. Growth in the emerging markets will generate massive transportation needs in the coming decades. Already the rush is on to stake out positions in China, India, and Latin America. But what form will this opportunity take?

Consider the potential impact of automobiles on China alone. Today there are fewer than 1 million cars on the road in China. However, with a population of more than 1 billion, it would take less than 30% market penetration to equal the current size of the U.S. car market (12 million to 15 million units sold per year). Ultimately, China might demand 50 million or more units annually. Because China's energy and transportation infrastructures are still being defined, there is an opportunity to develop a clean technology yielding important environmental and competitive benefits.

Amory Lovins of the Rocky Mountain Institute has demonstrated the feasibility of building *hypercars*—vehicles that are fully recyclable, 20 times more energy efficient, 100 times cleaner, and cheaper than existing cars. These vehicles retain the safety and performance of conventional cars but achieve radical simplification through the use of lightweight, composite materials, fewer parts, virtual prototyping, regenerative braking, and very small, hybrid engines. Hypercars, which are more akin to computers on wheels than to cars with microchips, may render obsolete most of the competencies associated with today's auto manufacturing—for example, metal stamping, tool and die making, and the internal combustion engine.

Assume for a minute that clean technology like the hypercar or Mazda's soon-to-be-released hydrogen rotary engine can be developed for a market such as China's. Now try to envision a transportation infrastructure capable of accommodating so many cars. How long will it take before gridlock and traffic jams force the auto industry to a halt? Sustainability will require new transportation solutions for the needs of emerging economies with huge populations. Will the giants in the auto industry be prepared for such radical change, or will they leave the field to new ventures that are not encumbered by the competencies of the past?

A clear and fully integrated environmental strategy should not only guide competency development, it should also shape the company's relationship to customers, suppliers, other companies, policymakers, and all its stakeholders. Companies can and must change the way customers think by creating preferences for products and services consistent with sustainability. Companies must become educators rather than mere marketers of products. (See the exhibit "Building Sustainable Business Strategies.")

For senior executives, embracing the quest for sustainability may well require a leap of faith. Some may feel that the risks associated with investing in unstable and unfamiliar markets outweigh the potential benefits. Others will recognize the power of such a positive mission to galvanize people in their organizations.

Regardless of their opinions on sustainability, executives will not be able to keep their heads in the sand for long. Since 1980, foreign direct investment by multinational corporations has increased from $500 billion to nearly $3 trillion per year. In fact, it now exceeds official development-assistance aid in developing countries. With free trade on the rise, the next decade may see the figure increase by another order of magnitude. The challenges presented by emerging markets in Asia and Latin America demand a new way of conceptualizing business opportunities. The rapid growth in emerging economics cannot be sustained in the face of mounting environmental deterioration, poverty, and resource depletion. In the coming decade, companies will be challenged to develop clean technologies and to implement strategies that drastically reduce the environmental burden in the developing world while simultaneously increasing its wealth and standard of living.

Like it or not, the responsibility for ensuring a sustainable world falls largely on the shoulders of the world's enterprises, the economic engines of the future. Clearly, public policy innovations (at both the national and international levels) and changes in individual consumption

Building Sustainable Business Strategies

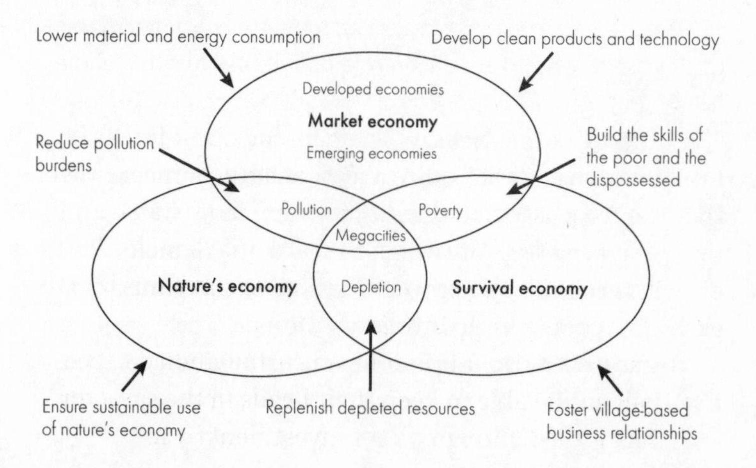

patterns will be needed to move toward sustainability. But corporations can and should lead the way, helping to shape public policy and driving change in consumers' behavior. In the final analysis, it makes good business sense to pursue strategies for a sustainable world.

Aracruz Celulose: A Strategy for the Survival Economy

"POVERTY IS ONE of the world's leading polluters," notes Erling Lorentzen, founder and chairman of Aracruz Celulose. The $2 billion Brazilian company is the world's largest producer of eucalyptus pulp. "You can't expect people who don't eat a proper meal to be concerned about the environment."[1]

From the very start, Aracruz has been built around a vision of sustainable development. Lorentzen understood that building a viable forest-products business in Brazil's impoverished and deforested state of Espirito Santo would require the simultaneous improvement of nature's economy and the survival economy.

First, to restore nature's economy, the company took advantage of a tax incentive for tree planting in the late 1960s and began buying and reforesting cut-over land. By 1992, the company had acquired over 200,000 hectares and planted 130,000 hectares with managed eucalyptus; the rest was restored as conservation land. By reforesting what had become highly degraded land, unsuitable for agriculture, the company addressed a fundamental environmental problem. At the same time, it created a first-rate source of fiber for its pulping operations. Aracruz's forest practices and its ability to clone seedlings have given the company advantages in both cost and quality.

Aracruz has tackled the problem of poverty head-on. Every year, the company gives away millions of eucalyptus seedlings to local farmers. It is a preemptive strategy, aimed at reducing the farmers' need to deplete the natural forests for fuel or lumber. Aracruz also has a long-term commitment to capability building. In the early years, Aracruz was able to hire local people for very low wages because of their desperate situation. But instead of simply exploiting the abundant supply of cheap labor, the company embarked on an aggressive social-investment strategy, spending $125 million to support the creation of hospitals, schools, housing, and a training center for employees. In fact, until recently, Aracruz spent more on its social investments than it did on wages (about $1.20 for every $1 in wages). Since that time, the standard of living has improved dramatically, as has productivity. The company no longer needs to invest so heavily in social infrastructure.

1. Marguerite Rigoglioso, "Stewards of the Seventh Generation," Harvard Business School Bulletin, April 1996, p. 55.

Notes

1. The terms *market economy, survival economy,* and *nature's economy* were suggested to me by Vandana Shiva, *Ecology and the Politics of Survival* (New Delhi: United Nations University Press, 1991).

Originally published in January–February 1997
Reprint 97105

Competitive Advantage on a Warming Planet

JONATHAN LASH AND FRED WELLINGTON

Executive Summary

WHETHER YOU'RE in a traditional smokestack industry or a "clean" business like investment banking, your company will increasingly feel the effects of climate change. Even people skeptical about global warming's dangers are recognizing that, simply because so many others are concerned, the phenomenon has wide-ranging implications.

Investors already are discounting share prices of companies poorly positioned to compete in a warming world. Many businesses face higher raw material and energy costs as more and more governments enact policies placing a cost on emissions. Consumers are taking into account a company's environmental record when making purchasing decisions. There's also a burgeoning market in greenhouse gas emission allowances (the carbon market), with annual trading in these assets valued at tens to billions of dollars. Companies that manage and mitigate their exposure to the risks associated with climate change while seeking new opportunities for profit will generate a competitive advantage over rivals in a carbon-constrained future.

This article offers a systematic approach to mapping and responding to climate change risks. According to Jonathan Lash and Fred Wellington of the World Resources Institute, an environmental think tank; the risks can be divided into six categories: *regulatory* (policies such as new emissions standards), *products and technology* (the development and marketing of climate-friendly products and services), *litigation* (lawsuits alleging environmental harm), *reputational* (how a company's environmental policies affect its brand), *supply chain* (potentially higher raw material and energy costs), and *physical* (such as an increase in the incidence of hurricanes). The authors propose a four-step process for responding to climate change risk: Quantify your company's carbon footprint; identify the risks and opportunities you face; adapt your business in response; and do it better than your competitors.

WHETHER YOU'RE in a traditional smokestack industry or a "clean" business like investment banking, your company will increasingly feel the effects of climate change. Even people skeptical of the dangers of global warming are recognizing that simply because so many others are concerned, the phenomenon has wide-ranging implications.

Investors already are discounting share prices of companies poorly positioned to compete in a warming world.

Many businesses face higher raw material and energy costs as governments around the globe increasingly enact policies placing a cost on emissions. Consumers are taking into account a company's environmental record when making purchasing decisions. There's a burgeoning market in greenhouse gas emission allowances (the so-called carbon market), with annual trading in these assets valued at tens of billions of dollars. Even in the United States, which has lagged the rest of the developed world in the regulation of greenhouse gas emissions, the debate is rapidly shifting from whether climate change legislation should be enacted to when and in what form.

Companies that manage and mitigate their exposure to climate-change risks while seeking new opportunities for profit will generate a competitive advantage over rivals in a carbon-constrained future. We offer here a guide for identifying the ways in which climate change can affect your business and for creating a strategy that will help you manage the risks and pursue the opportunities. We cite examples of very different companies—from Caterpillar to Wal-Mart to Goldman Sachs—that are responding to the various forces unleashed by the growing awareness among business leaders and consumers of the importance of climate change. Our message: It's not enough to do something; you have to do it better—and more quickly—than your competitors.

The Effects of Climate Change on the Planet

Let us stop here for a second and state our belief that climate change does in fact pose a serious problem for the world. The buildup of greenhouse gases in the atmosphere is changing the earth's climate at a rate unprecedented in history. The year 2005 was the warmest on record, and the ten warmest years have all occurred since 1980. Ice in the Arctic, the Antarctic, and Greenland is melting, and virtually all of the world's glaciers are shrinking.

Numerous studies suggest that the warming of the earth's oceans has resulted in more-powerful tropical storms, which generate their energy from warm ocean waters. For example, a U.S. government study released in May 2006 found that the warming of the tropical North Atlantic will contribute to more and stronger hurricanes. In fact, global data show that storms, droughts, and other weather-related disasters are growing more severe and more frequent.

These observed effects are the result of a roughly one-degree-Fahrenheit warming of the planet, an increase that would accelerate under current emission trends, thereby increasing the pace of physical and biological changes. (See "How Much Warmer Will It Get?" on page 132.) Half of the fossil fuels ever burned have been used since the end of World War II, and emissions continue to rise rapidly. In order to halt the buildup of greenhouse gases in the earth's atmosphere, global emissions would have to stop growing at all in this decade and be reduced by an astonishing 60% from today's levels by 2050.

The consequences for the planet of inaction on climate change are becoming clear. But what exactly are the business implications?

The Effects of Climate Change on Your Company

Executives typically manage environmental risk as a threefold problem of regulatory compliance, potential liability from industrial accidents, and pollutant release mitigation. But climate change presents business risks that are different in kind because the impact is global, the problem is long-term, and the harm is essentially irreversible. Furthermore, U.S. government policies have offered companies operating in the United States little guidance as to how environmental policy may change in the future. Ignoring the financial and competitive consequences of climate change could lead a company to formulate an inaccurate risk profile.

While this obviously has been the case for utilities and energy-intensive industries like chemical manufacturing, it now holds true for most industries. In fact, the most important distinctions to be made when considering environmental risk assessment aren't between sectors but within sectors, where a company's climate-related risk mitigation and product strategies can create competitive advantage.

Government regulators aren't the only ones monitoring individual companies for inadequate climate-related practices. Big investors are beginning to demand more disclosure from companies. For example, the Carbon Disclosure Project, a coalition of institutional investors representing more than $31 trillion in assets, annually requests information from large multinational companies about their climate-risk positioning. Its most recent report, released in 2006, showed a marked increase not only in the awareness of climate change on the part of the respondents but also in the best practices being developed to manage exposure to climate risk.

Similarly, investor coalitions are filing shareholder resolutions requesting more climate risk disclosure from companies. More than two dozen climate-related resolutions were filed with companies in the 2004 to 2005 period, triple the number from 2000 to 2001.

As Wal-Mart CEO Lee Scott told us, a corporate focus on reducing greenhouse gases as quickly as possible is a good business strategy: "It will save money for our customers, make us a more efficient business, and help position us to compete effectively in a carbon-constrained world."

The far-reaching effects of climate change on business become clearer when you start to think about the different kinds of risk—most of which can be transformed into opportunities—and how they could affect the value of your company.

REGULATORY RISK

This is the most obvious area of impact, whether it takes the form of regulating emissions of the products you make (for example, automobile emission limits for carmakers) or of the manufacturing process you use in creating those products. Companies in much of the world are already subject to the Kyoto Protocol, which aims to reduce carbon dioxide and other greenhouse gases by requiring developed countries—and, by extension, companies operating within those countries—to limit greenhouse gas emissions.

To meet Kyoto targets, the European Union's Emissions Trading Scheme, for example, grants companies *allowances* that authorize them to emit certain amounts of specified greenhouse gases. If a company's emissions are higher than its allotted allowances, it has to buy additional allowances from other companies. If its emissions are lower than its allotment, it can sell its unneeded allowances on the market. Companies can earn *credits,* which also give the holder the right to emit certain amounts of gases, by investing in emissions abatement projects outside their own organizations and even countries—as when, say, a French company invests in a wind-powered electricity generation project in Brazil. These credits can either be used to offset companies' own emissions or be sold on the market.

Even in the United States, which withdrew from the Kyoto Protocol, various regional, state, and local government policies increasingly affect companies. Seven northeastern states have adopted an agreement to cap carbon emissions from utilities and establish a carbon-trading scheme. (See "A U.S. Carbon Market" at the end of this article.) California has enacted regulations requiring that from 2008 to 2016, greenhouse gas emissions from new cars be reduced by 30% and has passed legislation to reduce total emissions to 1990 levels by 2020. A 2007 executive order also requires a reduction in the carbon content in motor fuels. Twenty states require utilities to obtain a percentage of the power they sell from renewable sources, and more than 218 U.S. cities have adopted programs to reduce emissions.

The U.S. government seems increasingly likely to take some sort of action, possibly in the near future. One 30-country survey, conducted by GlobeScan, shows that 76% of Americans believe global warming is a serious problem, and half believe it is a very serious one. (All the other countries surveyed except Kenya and South Africa reported even greater concern on the part of residents.) Numerous emission-reduction bills have been introduced in the U.S. Congress, and, although federal legislation is still at least several years away, U.S. companies' investments in capital equipment—from power plants to new buildings—represent financial commitments to

How Much Warmer Will It Get?

According to NASA, 2005 was the warmest year in over a century, and the ten warmest years have all occurred since 1980. The shrinking polar ice caps aren't the only apparent consequence: Storms, droughts, and other weather-related disasters–for example, epidemics, whose spread is correlated with temperature and moisture rates–are growing more severe and more frequent.

All that, and the planet has warmed only by roughly one degree Fahrenheit. Most climate models predict a three- to eight-degree rise in global average temperatures if atmospheric concentrations of greenhouse gases reach twice preindustrial levels, something that will happen by 2050 if current trends continue. All of those models show some risk (between 5% and 15%) that the temperature will rise significantly more than that. Furthermore, there is a risk of unknown magnitude that positive feedback mechanisms in the climate system–for instance, the release of methane from melting permafrost in northern Canada, which could contribute to global warming and further melting of the permafrost–will create sudden, nonlinear accelerations in warming.

Frequency of weather-related disasters

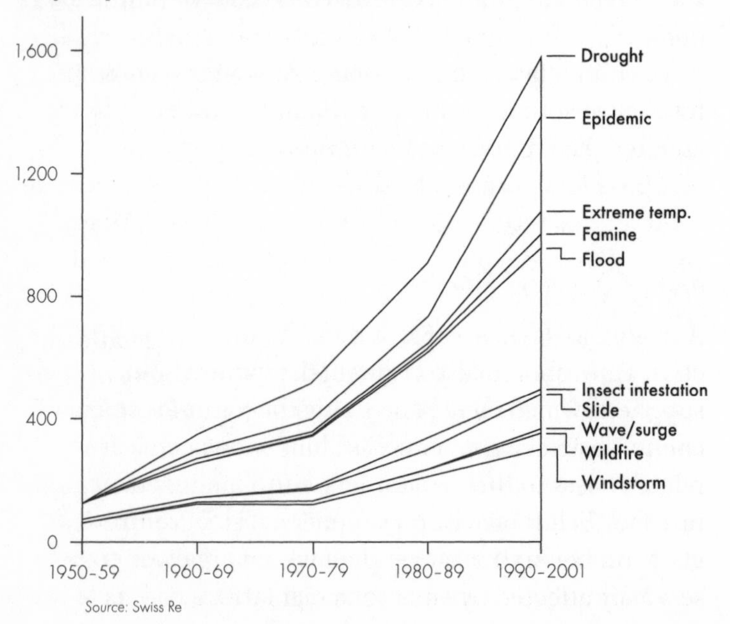

Source: Swiss Re

carbon dioxide emissions that may become very costly under future regulatory regimes.

For most businesses, a comprehensive federal policy concerning climate change is preferable to a patchwork of state and local regulations. Consequently, U.S. companies are beginning to shift their political position; more than 40 *Fortune* 500 companies have announced that they favor mandatory federal regulation of greenhouse gases. In January 2007, a group of leading companies, including Lehman Brothers, Alcoa, and Pacific Gas and Electric, called for rapid enactment of mandatory, economy-wide regulatory programs to support a 10% to 30% reduction of greenhouse gases over 15 years in the U.S. At a Senate hearing in 2006, representatives of companies such as General Electric, Duke Energy, and Exelon made the case that it was time to move forward with legislation. They would rather know the rules soon, they said, than be surprised by sudden political urgency.

By immediately initiating an assessment of how future legislation might affect them, companies can manage the regulatory risk and, crucially, gain an advantage over less prescient rivals.

SUPPLY CHAIN RISK

As they assess their susceptibility to future regulations, companies should also evaluate the vulnerability of their suppliers, which could lead to higher component and energy costs as suppliers pass along increasing carbon-related costs to their customers. Auto manufacturing, for instance, relies heavily on suppliers of steel, aluminum, glass, rubber, and plastics, all of whom are likely to be seriously affected by emissions regulations or—as in the case of aluminum manufacturing, a big consumer of energy—by regulations on their suppliers' suppliers.

A company should also take into account the geographical distribution of its supplier network. Executives should be aware of how many of their suppliers operate in, say, the European Union, where regulatory structures are already in place. In addition, executives must be mindful that the other climate-related risks discussed here could affect not just their own companies but their suppliers as well.

PRODUCT AND TECHNOLOGY RISK

Some companies will fare better than others in a carbon-constrained future, depending on their ability to identify ways to exploit new market opportunities for climate-friendly products and services.

For example, a technology for converting coal into energy (IGCC, or integrated gasification combined cycle), while currently more expensive than traditional methods used in pulverized-coal plants, can lower aggregate carbon emissions through better efficiency and possibly carbon dioxide capture and storage. In doing so, IGCC would reduce the significant costs that coal-fired plants would face under stricter emissions standards. Companies at the forefront of commercializing such technologies could see significant revenue growth as demand for low-carbon products increases.

Opportunities are not limited to the manufacturing sector. An investment management firm in the United Kingdom, Generation Investment Management, offers investment products that factor in the climate risks facing companies held in its portfolios. The insurance company AIG offers brokerage and greenhouse gas management services to clients participating in markets, such as the one operating in the European Union, for the buying and selling of greenhouse gas emissions allowances and credits.

Indeed, these new carbon markets create all kinds of opportunities for professional services firms, particularly financial institutions. Among other things, financial services firms can help companies craft the complex hedging and trading strategies needed to minimize costs in such markets.

LITIGATION RISK

Companies that generate significant carbon emissions face the threat of lawsuits similar to those common in the tobacco, pharmaceutical, and asbestos industries. For instance, in an unprecedented case spearheaded by the former New York attorney general Eliot Spitzer and currently being considered by the U.S. Second Circuit Court of Appeals, eight states and New York City have sued five of America's largest power companies, demanding that they cut carbon emissions. In a federal district court case in Mississippi, plaintiffs are suing oil and coal companies for greenhouse gas emissions, arguing that they contributed to the severity of Hurricane Katrina. The claims in that case include unjust enrichment, civil conspiracy (against the American Petroleum Institute), public and private nuisance, trespass, negligence, and fraudulent misrepresentation.

Companies that don't adequately address the issue of climate change also can create personal liabilities for directors and officers who become vulnerable to shareholder-related litigation. Swiss Re, for example, has found that such suits constitute a potential exposure in the company's directors and officers insurance portfolio.

REPUTATIONAL RISK

Companies also face judgment in the court of public opinion, where they can be found guilty of selling or using products, processes, or practices that have a negative impact on the climate. The potential for consumer or shareholder backlash is particularly high in environmentally sensitive markets or in competitive sectors where brand loyalty is an important attribute of corporate value. In a recent study analyzing the impact of climate change on brand value, The Carbon Trust, an independent consultancy funded by the UK government, found that in some sectors the value of a company's brand could indeed be at risk because of negative perceptions related to climate change. As is the case in other risk areas, companies can turn reputational risk into an opportunity by leveraging practices that show them to be good citizens of the planet.

PHYSICAL RISK

Finally, there is the direct risk posed by the changing climate itself: physical effects such as droughts, floods, storms, and rising sea levels. The insurance, agriculture, fisheries, forestry, real estate, and tourism industries are particularly exposed because of their dependence on the physical environment and the elements. Physical climate risk can also affect sectors such as oil and gas through higher insurance premiums paid on assets located in vulnerable areas. Munich Re, for instance, raised its rates for insuring Gulf Coast oil rigs by 400% in the days after Hurricane Katrina struck. And ripples of physical risk can extend into some unexpected areas: For instance, Coca-Cola studies the linkages between climate change and water availability and how this will impact the location of its new bottling facilities.

Because companies' exposure to each of these six aspects of climate risk differs greatly, it is essential to generate tailored climate-risk profiles and strategies to mitigate the risk. Of course, companies in a given sector will have similar exposure to certain risks. For example, regulatory risks are more important in the power sector, while supply chain risks are critical in retail industries. But there also are differences within sectors—for example, varying levels of reputational risk.

It's important to remember that for some industries there is a direct upside to climate change, because government policy and public concern will create new needs and new markets. For instance, the "green buildings" market has historically occupied a tiny niche in the construction industry. Now, rising energy prices and resurgent public concern about sustainability have transformed the markets for environmentally friendly materials and technologies into explosive growth areas. The National Association of Homebuilders, for instance, estimates that green buildings will account for 5% to 10% of housing starts in 2010, up from 2% in 2005.

The venture capitalist John Doerr was recently quoted as saying that green technology could match information technology and biotechnology as a significant money-making opportunity. He called climate change "one of the most pressing global challenges" and said that the resulting demand for innovation would create the "mother of all markets."

Improving Your Company's Climate Competitiveness

In working with firms as they assess their exposure to climate change and begin to develop climate strategies, we have found that the most successful efforts include four key steps, each of which requires strong leadership at the top and involves significant learning across the organization.

Step 1: Quantify your carbon footprint. Since you can manage only what you measure, companies need to first understand the source and level of their own greenhouse gas emissions and begin tracking those emissions over time. This quantitative and relatively straightforward task can lead to heightened consciousness of climate change issues within a company and set the stage for a broader look at the strategic risks and opportunities they pose.

In quantifying their carbon footprint, companies need to create an accurate inventory of their greenhouse gas emissions. They should differentiate between direct and indirect emissions—that is, between their own "smokestack" emissions and those resulting from their energy consumption, travel, and other activities. They should also establish and adjust emissions baselines and evaluate best practices in reporting this information. The aim is to identify and prioritize emission reduction opportunities and establish strategies for participating in greenhouse-gas-trading markets.

One method for performing this kind of accounting is the Greenhouse Gas Protocol, which our organization developed with the World Business Council for Sustainable Development. This tool, which has been taken up by the International Standards Organization, has been used by several hundred companies to measure and track their own greenhouse gas emissions and by industry groups, including the International Aluminum Institute and the International Council of Forest and Paper Associations, to develop complementary industry-specific calculation tools. (For a detailed explanation of how to use the protocol—along with a tool to help assess the value of emissions reduction initiatives and to factor climate-related costs into decisions on new capital projects—go to www.ghgprotocol.org.)

The pharmaceutical giant Pfizer has set guidelines requiring it to reduce its environmental footprint by lowering energy consumption. But that goal would be meaningless unless the company first created a systematic audit of its current activities that have a direct and indirect impact on greenhouse gas emissions. Having done that, the company can now identify possible conservation and emissions efficiency projects, which it reports through a companywide energy database. Pfizer has identified more than 600 such projects at all levels of the company.

Companies that quantify their footprints send a strong signal that they recognize the importance of climate change as a business risk—and an opportunity. We know of companies that began by conducting a carbon audit to uncover inefficient and costly energy practices and then moved on to identify opportunities for brand enhancement around the issue of climate change. As we'll see, these companies eventually leveraged their knowledge about climate-related issues to develop new and profitable products.

Step 2: Assess your carbon-related risks and opportunities. The emissions footprint tells only part of the story. After determining the direct and indirect impact your company is having on the climate, you need to broaden your analysis and think strategically about how the six risks could hurt—or offer opportunities that better position—your business.

The forest products company Weyerhaeuser, whose mills create a significant carbon footprint, has committed to reducing operational emissions by 40% by 2020. But the company should also be considering climate-related issues beyond its emissions profile. Will the transportation costs to deliver its products rise significantly in a carbon-constrained economy? Are there potential physical effects of climate change on its main raw material, trees, such as greater damage by wood beetles because of milder winters?

Another way to assess the effect that climate-related forces will have on your company is to consider their direct and indirect financial impact. You can look at the "carbon intensity" of your profits—that is, what percentage is derived from products with high carbon dioxide emissions. Or you can look at ways in which climate change could affect your revenues and costs. On the cost side, climate change may drive increases in raw material costs, direct regulatory costs, capital expenditures (for example, new facilities with lower emissions levels), insurance premiums for assets located in at-risk areas (such as the Gulf Coast), and possibly even new tax liabilities. Revenues will be affected by your ability to pass these costs on to customers through new pricing structures while exploiting new market opportunities and maintaining market share. (See "Climate Change and Profitability" at the end of this article.)

The interplay among the various elements of climate-related risk affects a firm's cost of capital and ultimately its valuation. Investors will factor a company's climate exposure into estimates of its future cash flow streams. The degree to which cash flow is sensitive to climate risk will also affect how much cash is available for interest expense and amortization of a company's debt, ultimately affecting its ratings on bonds and bank debt. Calculating the impact of climate risk on cash flows and costs of capital is critical to understanding your company's ability to compete in a carbon-constrained future.

Step 3: Adapt your business in response to the risks and opportunities. Having assessed the ways in which climate change could affect your company, you will be prepared to develop strategies and make moves based on that knowledge. Those moves range from the obvious reductions in energy consumption and carbon emissions to sometimes wholesale reinventions of parts of your business.

Caterpillar is investing in making its already relatively low-emission diesel engines more efficient. It also has found opportunity in the risk of greater regulation by building a new business that makes particulate filter systems to be retrofitted on its own and others' engines. The company is studying turbines that run on alternative fuels, as well as combined heat and power generation turbines that recover waste heat. It is poised to commit significant R&D funds to these projects as soon as U.S. regulations put a cost on carbon emissions, thus making alternative fuels and technologies more attractive.

Creative moves aren't restricted to heavy manufacturing and other industries traditionally unfriendly to the environment. Wal-Mart is in the middle of a three-year plan to reduce energy use at its stores by up to 30%. The initiative, part of a highly publicized plan to boost energy efficiency, cut down on waste, and reduce greenhouse gas emissions, was launched not only to meet current or anticipated regulations but to burnish the company's reputation in an area where it had been attacked by critics.

In a lower-emissions sector, financial services, another industry in which reputation is important, Goldman Sachs has implemented a coordinated environmental-policy framework that, among other things, requires the measurement and reporting of greenhouse gas emissions attributable to its internal operations. The firm also is active in the burgeoning market for carbon allowances and has a team dedicated to doing research for clients on how environmental issues such as climate change can affect stock market valuations. The company's stated aim for these programs: to boost earnings.

"We're committing people, capital, and ideas to find effective market-based solutions to some of the most critical challenges facing the planet," Mark Tercek, the managing director of the Goldman Sachs Center for Environmental Markets, told us. "We see this as being entirely consistent with our central business objective of serving our clients and creating long-term value for our shareholders."

Step 4: Do it better than your competitors. If Tercek is to be proved right, though, a "doing well by doing good" approach won't be enough: You have to be better at it than your competitors. And that means beating them in both areas: reducing exposure to climate-related risks and finding business opportunities within those risks.

Take the auto industry, which we have studied in detail. Consumer concerns about national energy security, climate change, local air pollution, and the cost of filling up at the pump are shaping the competitive dynamics within the industry. In mapping the climate competitiveness of the major automakers three years ago, we looked at two things: how well they were positioned vis-à-vis climate risk and how they were managing climate opportunities. The analysis found that Honda and Toyota were best positioned to sell cars in a carbon-constrained economy, not only because their current fleets were more fuel efficient than most of their rivals' but also because they were leaders in the commercialization of hybrid vehicles. GM and Ford were burdened with above-average cost exposure because of the high proportion of fuel inefficient vehicles like SUVs and pickup trucks in their product lines. (Even among these gas-guzzlers, carbon emissions vary by as much as 40%, with the U.S. automakers' models being the least fuel efficient.) Detroit's failure to develop innovative low-carbon technologies may be the greatest obstacle to their recovery. (For a look at how other automakers performed, using a matrix that could be applied to any industry, see the exhibit "Plotting Your Climate Competitiveness.")

General Electric has actively pursued competitive advantage through its climate policies. In 2003, it began using the Greenhouse Gas Protocol to construct an emissions inventory, allowing it to quantify its regulatory risk. It also joined a group of companies from different economic sectors—including Bristol-Myers Squibb, Citigroup, Con Edison, Johnson & Johnson, and Staples—to discuss climate strategies and learn from peers.

GE then began to think more strategically about how climate change could affect its business and that of its customers. In 2005, the company launched what it called Ecomagination, a coordinated product offering that features clean technologies that serve the transportation, energy, water, and consumer product sectors. GE's goals for the program were to double its annual investment in clean technologies to $1.5 billion by 2010 and to increase to at least $20 billion the revenue generated from products and services that offer customers measurable environmental performance advantages.

Plotting Your Climate Competitiveness

Reducing your exposure to climate risk and creating new opportunities for profit are both important steps in building your climate competitiveness. But if your competitors are doing these things better, your company is losing ground.

In 2003, we mapped the climate competitiveness of the ten largest global automakers, looking at their vulnerability to risks and their ability to seize opportunities. Our analysis was conducted with Sustainable Asset Management, an investment management firm. Specifically, we evaluated the vulnerability of each automaker's current product line to further fuel-economy regulation by calculating the estimated cost per vehicle to meet new emissions standards during the following decade. We also analyzed how well the companies were managing climate opportunities. Using a zero-to-100 scale, we qualitatively assessed how advanced each automaker was in its ability to commercialize, market, and mass-produce vehicles using one or more low-carbon technologies—hybrid battery-and-gasoline, for example, or fuel-cell technology. Perhaps not surprisingly, we found that Honda and Toyota were best positioned to sell cars in a carbon-constrained economy, both because their current fleets were relatively fuel efficient and because they were ahead of rivals in commercializing new technologies.

To determine where your company stands with respect to your competitors, you can map your own industry using these two variables—

GE is already well on its way to reaching perhaps the most critical element of this strategy: increasing profits. Revenues from Ecomagination products reached $10.1 billion in 2005, with orders and commitments nearing $17 billion. And the R&D program is already paying off, with a 75% increase in certified Ecomagination products brought to market.

The aggressive moves by GE and other forward-looking companies show that climate change isn't a topic to repeatedly table until next year's meeting. It is already influencing the competitive dynamics in markets all over the world. As GE chairman and CEO Jeffrey

---

positioning against risks and preparedness to seize opportunities. In doing so, you are likely to uncover ideas on how to move to a position of competitive advantage.

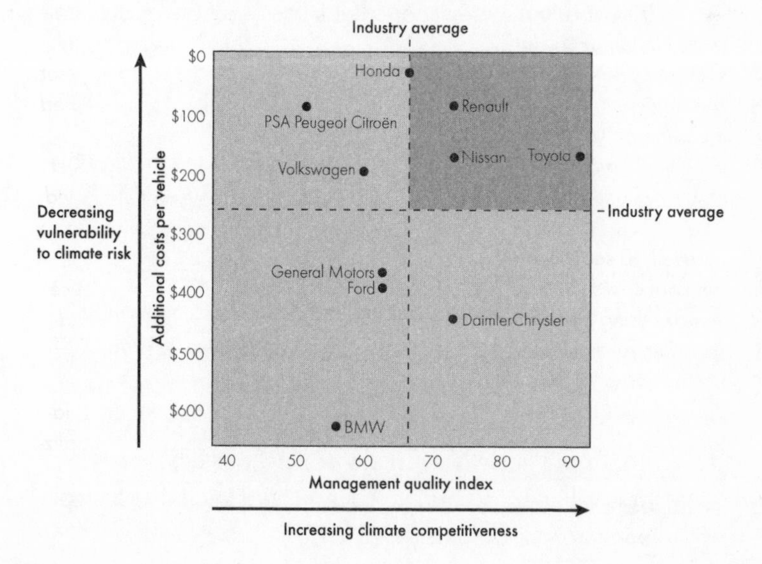

Immelt recently commented, "Our customers have made it clear that providing solutions to environmental challenges like climate change is essential to society's well-being, and a clear growth opportunity for GE. Companies with the technology and vision to provide products and services that address climate and other pressing issues will enjoy a competitive advantage." Or, to put it differently, they will do not just well but *better* by doing good.

A U.S. Carbon Market

THE EUROPEAN UNION'S MARKET that allows companies to buy and sell greenhouse gas emission credits granted under the Kyoto Protocol has received considerable attention. A similar kind of GHG market is beginning to form in the United States, at least on a regional basis, largely owing to the success of long-standing emissions trading systems for other kinds of air and water pollutants. The Regional Greenhouse Gas Initiative is a multistate government program aimed at reducing carbon dioxide emissions from power plants in the northeastern U.S. through a mix of emissions caps and the trading of emissions allowances. The initiative will govern GHG emissions from most electricity-generating units in the region that use more than 50% fossil fuel. Starting in 2009, and at the end of each three-year compliance period thereafter, each regulated source must own allowances equaling its aggregate carbon dioxide emissions during the period. Generating plants can buy, sell, bank, and trade allowances or purchase offset credits from other companies in ways that will keep their compliance costs as low as possible.

Climate Change and Profitability

ONE WAY TO LOOK at how climate-related forces will affect your company is to consider their impact on both costs and revenue. A company's ability to find opportunities in a carbon-constrained world will depend on its skill at hedging against physical climate risk, mitigating regulatory costs, avoiding expensive litigation and other threats to corporate reputation, managing climate risk in the supply chain, investing capital in low-carbon assets, and innovating around new technology and product opportunities.

Here are some prototype questions companies might ask themselves.

Potential Revenue Drivers

- How will changes in customer demand patterns affect pricing?
- What percentage of climate-related costs will we be able to pass through to customers?
- How can we generate streams of revenue from new low-carbon products?
- What new forms of income (for example, carbon credits) will become available?
- What threats do we face from low-carbon substitute products?
- What will be the impact of weather patterns on revenue?

Potential Cost Drivers

- How will regulatory policy affect our costs? (Will we need to purchase emissions allowances?)

- Is there a chance that emissions will also, or alternatively, be taxed?
- What capital expenditures do we face as a result of emissions-reduction plans?
- How much will our raw materials costs escalate? How much will those of our suppliers escalate?
- How much will our energy costs rise?
- How will our risk profile affect our insurance premiums?

Originally published in March 2007
Reprint R0703F

What Asbestos Taught Me About Managing Risk

BILL SELLS

Executive Summary

AS A MANAGER and executive with Johns-Manville, Bill Sells witnessed one of the greatest management blunders of the twentieth century. This blunder was denial, and in the end it took thousands of lives, destroyed an industry, and wiped out as much as 98% of stockholder equity.

From today's perspective, it hardly matters what and when Manville knew about asbestos. Modern liability standards seem to hold that the company *should* have known.

In 1968, Sells became manager of an asbestos-cement pipe plant whose low productivity and poor profits were blamed on poor labor relations. Gradually, he came to see that the plant had the labor relations it deserved. The factory was dingy, maintenance was slipshod, and dust-abatement standards were poorly enforced. The company had also neglected the safety of its downstream fabricators. Worst of all, managers suffered from the cynical conviction that change was impossible. Cleaning up the plant and changing attitudes produced a turnaround in productivity and profits, but by then, Manville had filed for Chapter 11 reorganization.

In the meantime, Sells was promoted to head Manville's fiberglass division, which, with asbestos virtually banned, had become its chief source of revenue. When fiberglass too came under suspicion as a health hazard, Sells used the lessons he had learned in asbestos to implement a policy of product stewardship: intensive workplace monitoring; full disclosure; assiduous communication with customers, workers, regulators, and the media; and an active scientific research program. Studies now indicate that fiberglass is safe. Sales and profits indicate that product stewardship is a source of competitive advantage.

As a manager with Johns-Manville and its successor, the Manville Corporation, for more than 30 years, I witnessed one of the most colossal corporate blunders of the twentieth century. This blunder was not the manufacture and sale of a dangerous product. Hundreds of companies make products more dangerous than asbestos—deadly chemicals, explosives, poisons—and the companies and their employees thrive. Manville's blunder was not even its frequently cited failure to warn workers and customers of what it knew to be the dangers of asbestos during the 1940s, when so much of the damage to workers' health was done. Given the exigencies of war and the widespread indifference to environmental dangers at that time, it would have taken more than warnings to prevent the tragedy.

In my opinion, the blunder that cost thousands of lives and destroyed an industry was a management blunder, and the blunder was denial. Asbestosis—a nonmalignant lung disease brought on by breathing asbestos fibers—had been known since the early 1900s, and the first indications of a connection between asbestos and lung cancer appeared in the 1930s. But Manville managers at every level were unwilling or unable to believe in the long-term consequences of these known hazards. They denied, or at least failed to acknowledge, the depth and persistence of management accountability.

Had the company responded to the dangers of asbestosis and lung cancer with extensive medical research, assiduous communication, insistent warnings, and a rigorous dust-reduction program, it could have saved lives and would *probably* have saved the stockholders, the industry, and, for that matter, the product. (Asbestos still has applications for which no other material is equally suited, and, correctly used, it could be virtually risk free.) But Manville and the rest of the asbestos industry did almost nothing of significance—some medical studies but no follow-through, safety bulletins and dust-abatement policies but no enforcement, acknowledgment of hazards but no direct warnings to downstream customers—and their collective inaction was ruinous.

The fundamental lesson I've learned in my 30 years in the asbestos and fiberglass industries is that, to be more than an empty gesture, responsibility must be overt, proactive, and farsighted. At Manville, denial became endemic to the corporate culture, so much so that even after top executives had recognized health and safety as a critical issue, many middle- and lower-level managers continued to hide behind rationalizations and the letter of what they took to be the law.

I am not going to write about what and when Manville managers knew or didn't know about the dangers of asbestos. In one sense, it hardly matters because the standard for product liability that I see applied today—partly as a result of the asbestos litigation—seems to build on the principle that companies are responsible for product hazards whether or not they knew about product dangers. This is a retroactive standard, of course, but it is the same standard we apply to every other management activity. We expect executives to anticipate and preevaluate market trends, capital requirements, staffing needs, research, new product developments, competitive pressures, and much, much more. We also expect them constantly to question their companies' practices and procedures. When executives fail to foresee the future at least enough to prevent business setbacks, they pay a penalty in compensation, promotion, or job security. Now juries and the courts demand no less in the area of product liability. For the New Jersey Supreme Court, not even "unknowability"—the absence of any scientific evidence that a product may be harmful—is an adequate defense.[1]

To protect employees, customers, stockholders, society, and the business itself from product and production hazards, managers must go well beyond appearances, union demands, and the letter of the law. They must anticipate and lead the drive to head off environmental hazards and risks. They must study, analyze, assess, communicate, and prevent the damage their methods and products might cause.

I am not speaking on some abstract moral plane. I learned these lessons the hard way, as a participating eyewitness to some of the worst outcomes a corporation can experience. Employees and customers suffered disabilities and died, and Manville was eventually required to help fund a personal-injury-settlement trust fund with $150 million in cash, $1.6 billion in bonds, 80% of the company's common stock, and, beginning in 1992 and continuing for as long as there are claims to settle, 20% of company profits.

Remarkably, however, my experiences as the manager of an asbestos plant and later as the head of Manville's fiberglass group also taught me that what is now called product stewardship—the active acceptance of product and production responsibility—yields short-term as well as long-term benefits, among them profit, survival, and even competitive advantage.

I went to work for Manville in June 1960, fresh from college and four years in the Marine Corps. When I joined it, Manville was the largest producer of asbestos products in the United States and the largest producer of asbestos fiber in the Western world, with 500 product lines and 33 plants and mines across the United States and Canada. To me, Manville seemed an ideal employer—an old-guard, blue-chip industrial giant, a member of the *Fortune* "500" and the Dow-Jones industrial average. "The bluest of the blue," *Forbes* once called it.

Since its founding in 1858, Manville had specialized in asbestos, a "miracle" substance with unique properties—fireproof, lightweight, durable, strong, an excellent insulator—that made it indispensable for hundreds of industrial and commercial applications. During World

War II, the government declared asbestos a strategic material, and its use mushroomed. So did its misuse. In wartime shipyards, workers installed asbestos below decks in conditions of intense heat and dust described by one eyewitness as a glimpse of hell. Even outside the shipyards, asbestos plants and fabricating shops tolerated dust standards that were later shown to be far too high.

Later, often decades later, the people who worked in those plants, shops, and shipyards began to develop asbestos-related diseases, including several forms of cancer. Tens of thousands were disabled or died. Claims that they and their survivors brought against the company came to hundreds of millions of dollars. In 1982, Manville filed for Chapter 11 protection and was on its way to the top of *Fortune*'s list of least admired corporations. The company was reorganized in 1988, and its stockholders—many of them Manville workers or retired workers—lost as much as 98% of their equity.

In 1960, I was ignorant of company history; I knew very little about the dangers of the product, which few employees understood well and still fewer discussed; and of course I had no inkling of the future. I started in sales, moved to marketing, and then, in 1968, I switched to production as a manager in training. After some brief hands-on experience as a supervisor at the Manville, New Jersey, plant, I packed up my family and headed for Waukegan, Illinois, to see if I could turn around a plant that made asbestos-cement pipe and ranked at the bottom of the heap in both productivity and profit.

The plant lay at the back of a sprawling complex built in the 1920s, its view of Lake Michigan obscured by a landfill several stories high. The road wound through this mountain of asbestos-laden scrap, and as I drove it for the first time, I stopped to watch a bulldozer crush a 36-inch sewer pipe. A cloud of dust swirled around my car.

Corrugated asbestos-cement panels covered the outside of the nearly windowless building. Inside, a forklift picked up a pallet of finished couplings and moved off in the dingy light, leaving a trail of dust. People told me things had improved. At one time, they said, you couldn't see from one end of the building to the other. But I saw asbestos dust on every ledge and purlin, and I wondered what I had gotten myself into.

Waukegan was a grueling experience right from the start. In sales, when you stop work, the selling function stops. In a continuous manufacturing operation, the machines keep running and endless problems devour every moment, night and day. Whenever the phone rang at home, I would hold my breath until I knew it wasn't someone calling from the plant. No one ever called with good news.

The task I'd been set was to increase productivity, but over the next two years, I discovered that low productivity had its roots in more basic problems. For example, conventional wisdom had it that the plant's poor performance was due to poor labor relations and a recalcitrant union that blocked productivity improvements. The truth, I learned, was a good deal more complex. For one thing, the plant's profit squeeze had caused previous managers to defer proper maintenance, which greatly increased downtime. For another, the lack of proper maintenance in the area of dust control was seriously affecting employee behavior. For a third, Manville's management culture had developed an unhealthy streak of cynicism. Too many engineers and middle managers had come to the conclusion—incorrectly, as events were to show—that workers were necessarily a part of the problem and not of the solution, that money could not be found for adequate upkeep, and that change was impossible.

Sometimes just by chance, sometimes by self-education and determination, sometimes in sheer desperation, I managed to turn most of this conventional wisdom on its head. But my learning curve was a series of painful shocks and confrontations.

To begin with, I lost my innocence about asbestos-related diseases. I encountered several new words: *dusted, red case,* and *mesothelioma. Dusted* was a shop-floor term for a person incapacitated by asbestosis. Severe lung changes, identified by X ray during physical examinations, were called *red cases.* When the doctor found changes like these, he would direct me to assign the worker in question to a "nondusty" area, which was a good deal easier said than done.

People at the plant seldom talked about asbestos diseases. Everyone knew who had high past exposures, and there was dismay but no surprise when a dusted worker got lung cancer. In the early 1960s, however, a new disease called mesothelioma struck several people who were not red cases. It was hard enough for people to get used to the progressive nature of asbestos-related diseases and learn to live with the possibility of permanent disability or death. Mesothelioma, a cancer of the lung or stomach lining, was a new and even more insidious threat. It came without warning; it sometimes occurred in people whose asbestos exposure had been minimal; and it was swift, untreatable, excruciating, and invariably fatal.

Deaths had already begun to occur in the workforce by the time I arrived in Waukegan, and I came to be a regular visitor at Victory Memorial Hospital. A young man just 25 years old, with a wife and children, died of mesothelioma. Others developed lung cancer. I got to know the doctor who treated most of these cases, and I started borrowing his medical journals and read dozens of articles on the subject. I began paying more and more attention to dust collection and abatement, hoping to bring Waukegan up to the standard of more modern plants. I pushed dust-reduction programs, and I organized a cleanup of inaccessible ledges and hard-to-reach beams and sills to reduce the levels of background dust. I even started wearing my own respirator in high-exposure areas, though, like everyone else, I was not nearly skeptical enough about the levels then considered "safe."

One memory still haunts me. Early one morning, I stopped at the hospital to see one of our lathe operators with mesothelioma only to be told that he had died a few hours before. The family was upstairs, and my heart was pounding as I walked into the room, acutely aware of my role as representative of the management system responsible for this premature death. The man's wife had known for months that this day was coming, but the finality of death and the uncertainty of the future were written all over her face. Her young son stared solemnly at her and then at me. I managed a few words of thin comfort, but I still remember the woman's face and my own feeling of helplessness.

A few days later, I learned that another plant in the Waukegan complex was going to close for good, and that set me up for another stark realization: our workers lived with two quite different kinds of fear.

The announcement was set for 11:30 A.M., and I arrived early. Clearly, the word was out. Groups of employees stood around talking, and I headed for the conference room as quickly as I could. Turning to go up the stairs, I found a man old enough to be my father sitting by himself with tears streaming down his cheeks. His face too came to haunt me over the years. People might dread the possibility of lung cancer or mesothelioma, but they also dreaded the possibility of losing the very jobs that put them at risk. And it was my responsibility to protect them from either outcome.

As this realization sank in, however, I began to see that these two responsibilities did not have to be at odds with each other. On the contrary, they were closely related, just like my two business goals.

My primary business mission in Waukegan was to improve plant profitability; my secondary objective was to gain union cooperation and support. Since people rarely do their best work for an employer who neglects their welfare, an improvement of environmental conditions was clearly essential to achieving either end. This seems like common sense today, but it was not accepted wisdom in the late 1960s.

Labor relations, productivity, dust abatement, profitability, health and safety—it struck me that at some level these were all the same issue. If there was anything at all I really wanted to know about the plant, the answer was always somewhere on the shop floor—perhaps not in one place or with one individual or in sophisticated technical terms, but there nonetheless. By getting to know more of the workers and more about their work, I realized that key operating indicators like downtime, material usage, quality, and productivity were as much a function of attitudes as they were of mechanics. I remembered what I'd been told about recalcitrant unions, and I suddenly saw that we had the labor relations we deserved.

Another piece of conventional thinking that plagued the Waukegan pipe plant was the whole question of maintenance.

Despite its early neglect of the problem, Manville had become a pioneer in industrial dust collection by the late 1940s. It had developed what were in effect gigantic vacuum cleaners with hundreds of dust filters and dozens of dust lines reaching out to dust hoods on every machine in virtually every corner of the plant. When profits got tight, unfortunately, Waukegan managers began to defer maintenance, and, in the early days, I took the same dead-end approach. Instead of replacing a damaged dust line, we mended it with duct tape. Instead of replacing or rebuilding a dust collector, we sent mechanics to shovel their way in every weekend and jerry-rig repairs. Soon we were spending most of our time retaping the tape and repairing the repairs, which put the maintenance curve out in front of us to stay. I watched us repeat the same repairs over and over again when the only real problem was the lack of proper repairs to begin with.

For more than a year, I was captive to the conventional notion that equipment that doesn't make a product makes no contribution to profit, but slowly I changed my mind. First, I saw that a cleaner plant would function more smoothly and help to reduce downtime. Then, as the morale and productivity benefits of a better plant environment became more and more apparent, I became a convert to the idea of cleanliness for its own sake. Finally, early one Sunday morning toward the end of my second year, the plant engineer and the production superintendent called me in to examine a massive breakdown. It was clear to all three of us that we couldn't go on the way we had, and pretty soon we were walking through the plant with a pad of paper, making a long list of everything that needed fixing. The list included a massive general cleanup.

We had already taken steps to reduce airborne fiber levels and clear away the accumulated dust of decades, but there was much still to do. The plan called for large investments in maintenance and dust-collecting capacity as well as dozens of practical improvements. We described in detail all the environmental improvements we required and presented our analysis to the division staff in Manville, New Jersey. They offered practical suggestions, private advice that I not try to do everything at once, and the cynical prediction that if I were foolish enough to present the plan to top management, I'd get tossed out on my ear.

In fact, top management knew more than middle management about the importance of environmental quality. At my next semiannual meeting with chairman and CEO Clinton Burnett and members of his staff, I conducted a tour of the plant and then laid out my plan, complete with charts and drawings. Or at least I started to. Before I had finished, Burnett interrupted to ask how much the whole thing was going to cost. With only the tiniest catch in my voice, I told him half a million dollars. "Fine," he said, turning to his staff. "Does anyone have a problem with that?"

With our capital expenditures approved, we proceeded to rebuild, replace, clean, or otherwise refurbish nearly everything in the building. We made big improvements and thousands of small ones. We installed experimental cardboard dust hoods to test for effective configurations before fabricating permanent hoods of metal. We repaired our dust collectors thoroughly and properly, and we installed air locks and built stairs in place of ladders.

As dust counts fell, so did our costs. We had probably made not a single change that someone hadn't thought of years earlier; the difference was that now we were actually making them. As a result, people began to identify other problems and fix them. The plant's productivity rose. People seemed to *care* more than they had before.

But even as we turned the corner on productivity and began to win our own small battle to save Waukegan from closing, the war as a whole was already lost. Negative public perception of asbestos was growing, and the market was beginning to crumble. By the late 1970s, asbestos plants were closing down right and left. In 1982, Manville filed for Chapter 11 reorganization, which was finally granted in 1988.

Our ultimate acknowledgment of the asbestos problem in the 1980s, which even then was grudging and half-hearted in some parts of the company, had come 50 years too late. During the 1970s and 1980s, I had to say good-bye to every member of my Waukegan administrative staff. They had become my friends, and now, one by one, they contracted mesothelioma and died.

In retrospect, it seems self-evident that clean air and a clean environment should have top priority in asbestos plants, especially in plants where some workers have already fallen ill and even died from asbestos-related diseases. But all through the decades of the 1940s, 1950s, and 1960s, managers skirted many of the real issues and gave surprisingly short shrift to others. Denial is itself an insidious disease. Once given a toehold, it finds its way into management acts and decisions at every level.

For example, it was common practice in Waukegan to test for dust under the best possible circumstances to make the plant look good on paper. It took a lecture by a medical expert at a plant managers' meeting to make me see that the only way to monitor dust emissions meaningfully was to test our *dirtiest* products and equipment under the *worst* conditions, which is exactly what we began to do in about 1970, when we implemented our grand environmental plan.

Another thing I often saw people do was hide behind procedures and standards when common sense would have served them better as a guide. I remember writing a request for funds to repair a dust hood on a coupling lathe and having one of my engineers attach a report stating that he had tested the area and found dust levels within company guidelines. There was nothing *wrong* with his report. Procedurally it was quite correct. But just to make sure my request would be approved, I took his pen and wrote on the report that I could see dust in the area.

If an organization's culture encourages denial, problems get buried. Corporate cultures are built by successful people, good men and women who are often pillars of their communities as well as business leaders. The executives at Manville were good people too, and nevertheless they fostered a culture of self-deception and denial. Consider all the various forms this took:

First was the conviction that asbestos was inherently useful, necessary, and therefore "good." I remember hearing colleagues argue that the world could never get along without it; substitutes were not economically viable and never would be. Today 18 asbestos companies have filed for bankruptcy, asbestos is effectively eliminated from commerce, and asbestos-free substitutes exist for every former use.

Another powerful form of denial was the conviction that we were already doing everything possible to reduce risk. Manville acknowledged that the product was potentially harmful but insisted that employees, unions, customers, regulators, scientists, and insurance companies all knew of the dangers. Furthermore, we had modern dust-collection equipment and a standard for airborne fibers that bettered the national standard at the time by half. We also issued regular bulletins about acceptable procedures and exposure levels. What more could we possibly do?

I have already shown how that attitude led to a pernicious form of self-deception in some older facilities like Waukegan, where cost consciousness or an individual manager's failure to think ahead led to ineffective dust abatement. But even at the new plants, where state-of-the-art equipment really did keep dust to a minimum, we might have asked whether our airborne-fiber standards were really adequate. True, in the late 1960s, the allowable limit set by the American Conference of Governmental Industrial Hygienists was 12 fibers per cubic centimeter and Manville's was 6. But did we know that number was low enough? Were we funding research to find out? The answer is no. By 1972, OSHA had set its standard at 5 fibers per cc and then lowered it to 2 in 1976. By 1986, even 2 had been reduced 90% to an allowable level of 0.2 fibers per cc.

Worse yet, while environmental standards in most Manville plants were perhaps low enough to protect our own workers, there was a big additional health problem farther downstream in fabricating shops and among people installing asbestos products like brake shoes.

A third form of denial was the tendency to believe that the fault lay elsewhere. During World War II, for example, the U.S. government controlled the use and applications of asbestos as a strategic and critical war material. Surely the government should bear some responsibility for the ensuing problems. The government eventually escaped responsibility by claiming "sovereign immunity," but that claim might have failed if Manville had assumed more responsibility at the time—during the war—and tried to persuade the shipyards to improve working conditions. Protests might not have solved the problem—with ships burning and sinking almost daily, those in charge clearly put production ahead of potential long-term health hazards—but a paper trail of responsible warnings could have saved the company by involving the government in subsequent product liability claims.

Another potential scapegoat was tobacco. In 1979, a study revealed that asbestos workers who smoked suffered 50 times more asbestos-related lung cancer than those who did not. Surely the tobacco industry too should share responsibility. Ironically, the cigarette manufacturers found refuge in the government-mandated warning labels that have served them as a defense against product liability claims.

A fourth form of denial derives from the very nature of corporations. Companies exist to go on existing, and corporate existence is a matter of monthly and quarterly goals. Manville managers never knowingly took any action that placed their customers or stockholders at risk over the short term. The long-term consequences of their actions were another matter.

Finally, there is a form of denial called "Don't tell me what I don't want to hear." Early in my career, my boss chided me because I strongly disagreed with him on some issue. "Bill, you're not loyal," he said. And I said, rightly, I think, "No, no, you've got it wrong. I'm the one who *is* loyal."

Every CEO needs to remember that what he or she knows is only a small part of the legal equation. Today's legal standard also convicts people for what they *should have known.* Manville did not violate the written law, but juries found that the company did violate the public trust. *Caveat vendor* has replaced *caveat emptor* in the courts.

In 1972, I left Waukegan for Manville's Denver headquarters to manage all Manville pipe production; in 1974, I became general manager of the industrial products division; and in 1978, I was appointed vice president for production and engineering. Then, in 1981, I took charge of the Fiber Glass Manufacturing Division. Predictably, I encountered dozens of large and small production headaches, but after years of dealing with health issues in the asbestos business, it was a joy to tackle normal business problems again.

Fiberglass was by then the leading profit producer in the company. Although widely seen as an alternative to asbestos, fiberglass is, in fact, only a partial substitute. Like asbestos, fiberglass will not burn, but it will melt at high enough temperatures. Like asbestos, fiberglass is an excellent insulator, but it will not stand up to the intense wear and other demanding applications that gave asbestos such industrial value.

Fiberglass differed from asbestos in another critical respect as well. Despite more than 40 years of scientific studies, there was little evidence connecting fiberglass to anything more serious than irritation from prolonged exposure. Most recently, in the early 1980s, a government laboratory in Los Alamos, New Mexico, had carried out an inhalation study using laboratory animals, which gave fiberglass a completely clean bill of health. Even lung irritation from the high experimental dosages appeared to be completely reversible once the animal was removed from the exposure. After more than 20 years with asbestos, I was now dealing with a truly benign substance.

Of course, we were taking no chances. The environmental controls in our fiberglass plants were well maintained and extremely effective, and workplace monitoring was routine. The product also carried a warning label about the potential for irritation.

During the early 1980s, Manville consolidated fiberglass marketing and manufacturing into a single Fiber Glass Group, and I became group president. Encouraged by Dr. Bob Anderson, who was Manville's corporate medical director, I became a strong proponent of aggressive scientific research.

In October 1986, Bob was in Copenhagen attending a symposium on man-made mineral fibers chaired by Sir Richard Doll, a world-renowned epidemiologist. The conference was uneventful until its last few moments. In his concluding remarks, Doll summarized the most important presentations and then ended with this comment: "If I now abandon the firm basis of scientific judgment . . . I do so because I know that, in the absence of such a conclusion, many people may think that the whole symposium has been a waste of time. Let me therefore add . . . accepting that [fiberglass and other man-made mineral fibers] are not more carcinogenic than asbestos fibers, we can conclude that exposure to fiber levels of the order of 0.2 respirable fibers per [cubic centimeter] is unlikely to produce a measurable risk even after another 20 years have passed."

Confirming the fact that low exposure to man-made mineral fibers would not produce measurable risk was not news, and exposures, especially in fiberglass, were extremely low. But 0.2 was the *asbestos* standard. What Doll had done was to establish a link between a known carcinogen and fiberglass!

Bob called me immediately, and the first words out of his mouth were, "Bill, our lives may have just changed forever." We both knew from experience that once a public perception is created, changing it can be extremely difficult. I hung up the phone and thought, I don't deserve two of these in one lifetime.

The best scientific and health information available indicated to us that fiberglass posed little if any risk to workers or users. But wasn't it possible that Manville executives reached the same conclusion about asbestos in the 1930s? I leaned back in my chair, ran through all the perceived failings of the asbestos industry in my head, and compared them to the situation we were now facing with fiberglass.

Had we done enough scientific research? Were our environmental controls and conditions the best in the world? Had workplace monitoring given us an accurate assessment of risk for factory workers as well as fabricators and installers? Had our audits found all the environmental and safety problems? And were we fixing these problems as soon as we found them?

I kicked myself mentally on realizing that our score wasn't an A+ but, unfortunately, more like a B. If anyone should have known better, it was I. But at least there was no question about what we had to do now. First and foremost, we were going to communicate.

Manville's new president, Tom Stephens, was well schooled in the roots of the asbestos tragedy. Like me, he had learned more than a little about corporate denial and more than a lot about corporate responsibility.

Within hours, we had posted Doll's remarks on all plant bulletin boards and begun the process of communicating with all our customers, first by phone and then in person. This was the first move in a communications campaign that continued for years, to the mystification of many. From the start, for example, our fiberglass competitors criticized us for not thinking through what they called the "probable impact of our actions." But we did think them through. Our competitors did not understand the history of asbestos.

Doll's remarks were only the first of many challenges. In June 1987, the International Agency for Research on Cancer (IARC) met in France, debated human and animal scientific studies separately, and concluded that the human evidence was not sufficient to consider fiberglass a possible cause of lung cancer. But on the basis of animal implantation work—glass fibers that were surgically implanted directly into the body cavities of laboratory rats—and over the protests of scientists who felt that inhalation tests were more accurate predictors of a potential hazard, the IARC classified fiberglass wool as "possibly carcinogenic to humans."

The IARC cautions that its findings are not to be considered assessments of risk, but the difference between hazard and risk is often confusing. Hazard defines the potential to produce harm; risk reflects the probability that this hazard will be realized. For example, radiation is hazardous, but when your dentist covers you with a lead shield and takes low-dosage X rays, there is little if any risk. The IARC is chartered to assess hazard only. By U.S. law, however, IARC findings automatically trigger a lot of state and federal product-safety regulations, and the trigger goes off without any risk assessment. Moreover, the regulations require companies to communicate the hazard, not the risk. Outside of scientific circles, these rules create a great deal of confusion.

In October 1987, the International Program on Chemical Safety (IPCS) of the World Health Organization declared that animal-inhalation studies were the most relevant way of assessing potential hazards to human beings. That finding agreed with our own convictions on the subject, but it would take several years to complete new studies and several more for the IARC to consider the new evidence.

We included the IARC finding in our product literature and added a "possible cause of cancer" warning label on all fiberglass-wool products.

"I will tell you the truth," I told all our customers, "and if I don't know, I will tell you I don't know, along with what I am doing to find out." Put very simply, our communications policy was, "You'll know when we know." We gave regular briefings on fiberglass safety and health to customers, employees, union officials, community leaders, and regulatory agencies by phone, letter, brochure, videotape, live television, and group meetings.

If there wasn't one crisis, there were three. We finally realized that truth, like beauty, was in the eye of the beholder. Regulatory agencies, the media, nonfiberglass competitors, and the fiberglass industry—all interpreted the truth to serve themselves. At the time, I didn't understand this aspect of the problem, and it led to conflict and frustration. Take the regulatory agencies:

The IPCS conclusion that inhalation was the preferred method for assessing a potential hazard led the fiberglass industry to fund a new inhalation study. We assembled a panel of independent scientists in Denver, and for two days they hammered out a protocol to achieve the highest possible scientific standard for the study. Then we signed a contract with a laboratory in Geneva, the only one in the world that met the panel's quality standards.

We sent the protocols to the appropriate regulatory bodies in advance of the study and routinely briefed them on its progress. After two years, the tests concluded with entirely negative results—*no* evidence that respirated fiberglass fibers affected the rate of lung cancer in laboratory rats. We were elated.

But the regulatory agencies did not find the results as conclusive as we did. Scientific conclusions are based on assumptions—change the assumptions, and you get a different conclusion—and the protocols and assumptions of this study were industry's, not OSHA's or the EPA's. The scientists who consulted for us had designed an extensive chronic-inhalation study using state-of-the-art inhalation technology. We knew that a positive finding would establish fiberglass as a hazardous substance, and while we didn't expect that outcome, we were prepared for the possibility. We were not prepared for the regulators' response to a negative finding, which seemed merely to arouse their automatic skepticism about industry intentions. They seemed to feel that a study that found no hazard in the product could not, by definition, be "most protective" of society.

It taught us that we should have involved the regulators in the formulation of assumptions and protocols. A negative finding that was based on their own assumptions would have been more difficult for them to pick apart.

The media presented another challenge. When the inhalation study came in with negative results, we declared victory in our internal publications and wanted the media to do the same. We continuously presented our view of truth to the press by explaining the IARC's hazard-assessment process, the difference between hazard and risk, the physical differences between asbestos and fiberglass, and our conviction that fiberglass posed little if any risk to workers. But reporters are even more suspicious than regulators. By adding our own side of the story to every disclosure, we managed to convince them they were getting less than the whole truth. As a result, they grasped at any source of negative information or simply reminded their readers of the IARC's original classification. We got headlines like, "Evidence Grows on Possible Link of Fiberglass and Lung Illness" or "Could Fiberglass Become the Asbestos of the 1990s?" The lesson that taught me was never to give in to pressure to try to make ourselves look good in risk communications. Let public relations do that work for itself. In risk communications, stick to the facts.

Nonfiberglass competitors were yet another problem. Our candid communication policy delighted many of them. The more we disclosed, the more information they had to twist and distort with customers. The issue also gave them an umbrella to put some new competitive products on the market (none of which, by the way, were subjected to hazard or risk assessment). We had to use legal means to stop the most blatant distortions, and most attempts to sensationalize the issue backfired. Our best weapon was our communication policy itself, because most customers understood that we were telling them everything we knew.

We learned that truth is relative, but we also learned that a consistent, conscientious commitment to the truth is a weapon powerful enough to overcome relativity, cynicism, and a great deal of fear. Driven by business as well as liability concerns, our customers wanted us to keep them up-to-date, and that was a perfect fit with our you'll-know-when-we-know policy. As customers began to depend on us for the latest news on fiberglass and health, relationships steadily improved, and I started receiving letters from customers supporting our actions. Our policy was so effective that its critics changed their tune from "You are going to destroy the industry" to "You must be doing this to gain competitive advantage."

Through all the turmoil and adverse publicity, fiberglass has remained the preferred material for residential insulation and has retained or improved its market position in the industrial, commercial, filtration, and aerospace segments. In fact, 1993 was one of the best sales years in the history of the fiberglass-wool industry.

In its product liability defense, the asbestos industry argued that it did not violate the law. The law required no warnings; a supplier's liability was limited to simple negligence. Moreover, the medical data were not conclusive until the 1960s. While technically correct, this defense was tied to the legalities of the past, and in the mid-1970s, with the benefit of hindsight, juries began to make judgments on the basis of what companies should have done, should have known, and should have disclosed. Increasingly, they judged the asbestos industry guilty of not meeting this new, higher, retroactive standard and required it to pay punitive damages for its failure to do so.

When I learned to fly an airplane on instruments, I was taught that my senses were always wrong and that the instruments were always right. As managers, our senses are finely tuned to deal with short-term changes and seldom help us with the blind landings that are still years away. When the pressure to cut short-term costs is high, it simply goes against the grain to increase spending for environmental controls with an uncertain long-term payback. What I learned as a businessman in the asbestos and fiberglass industries was that the instruments of long-term guidance are called principles. More specifically, they're called responsibility and product stewardship.

Product stewardship—defined as product responsibility extending through the entire stream of commerce, from raw material extraction to the ultimate disposal of a used-up or worn-out product—can cost a lot of money. But so can the alternative. Moreover, product stewardship probably represents the legal standard of tomorrow. Environmental regulations grow steadily tougher, and the imputed knowledge from these regulations will almost certainly carry over into the area of product liability.

I cannot possibly say how many companies are putting themselves and their employees and customers at this kind of risk today. I think I do know that voluntary product stewardship adds up to competitive advantage over the short term and a greatly improved chance of survival and profit into the future.

Notes

1. *Beshada v. Johns-Manville Products Corp.,* 90 N.J. 191, 447 A. 2d 539 (1982).

Originally published in March–April 1994
Reprint 94209

The Case of the Environmental Impasse

ALISSA J. STERN

Executive Summary

EVEN IN AN INDUSTRY notorious for polluting rivers and clear-cutting vast amounts of woodland, Vermilion Paper Company long had a reputation for environmental insensitivity. But in the mid-1980s, Vermilion began to see the green writing on the wall. Peter Ostenson, director of offshore production, was one of a new generation of managers partly responsible for this change in attitude. After selling Vermilion's skeptical CEO, Oliver Hibbing, on a strategy combining the business and environmental agendas, Ostenson set his sights on starting a eucalyptus plantation in the country of Equitania.

Ostenson chose Wendell Buyck, a young and like-minded manager, to head the effort. With little foreign experience, Buyck had his work cut out for him, first in gaining Equitanian government approval and then meeting the demands of provincial officials. But Buyck went one unprecedented step farther by calling a meeting with Equitanian environmentalists, who, after tense negotiations, agreed to take a position of "nondisapproval."

But six weeks later, a renegade Equitanian environmental group and a militant U.S. group launched a campaign to discredit Vermilion. An ad appearing in four U.S. newspapers accused the company of exploiting the Third World; later, the groups threatened to boycott Vermilion products if the company didn't halt its Equitanian project.

Vermilion's choices seemed stark. Ostenson argued that the company should stay and fight, but Hibbing wasn't interested: "Millions and millions of people haven't seen these ads. And if we write off this fairly small investment, they never will."

Four experts on business and the environment examine Vermilion's options and debate its next move.

ENVIRONMENTALISTS OF EVERY STRIPE disliked the Vermilion Paper Company. Even in an industry notorious for pumping rivers full of noxious waste and clear-cutting woodlands in county-sized chunks, Vermilion had a reputation for insensitivity. At one time or another, almost every jurisdiction in which it owned forests or mills had taken legal action against it for violating some environmental statute. In the 1970s, one of its own major stockholders sued the company for polluting a river the man liked to fish in.

Recently, however, Vermilion management had begun to see the green writing on the wall. The retirement of several executives who had begun their careers at a time when many people accepted pollution as a condition of progress had made way for fresh ideas and a more "socially responsible" manufacturing and marketing strategy. Moreover, consumers still associated the Vermilion name with good paper products at a good price and knew little or nothing of the company's shabby environmental record, so it was not too late to change course.

On the other hand, it was none too soon. Over the past five years, several international environmental groups had organized a campaign called Vermilion Action to inform the public about Vermilion's record and bring pressure to bear on the company to clean up its act. If environmentalists continued to target Vermilion as a public enemy, sooner or later the image would begin to stick.

In the mid-1980s, the company launched a campaign to change its image. Essentially a marketing effort, the campaign was built around the slogan "Green Vermilion" and consisted primarily of television ads and bright green labels on every bright red package of tissue and paper towels proclaiming environmentally friendly products and policies. For example, the company made much of the fact that it did not cut virgin forest, though in fact it had not cut any virgin forest in the United States since the mid-1940s, when it ran out of virgin forest to cut and went to tree farms. The green labels also declared in large type that the product inside was biodegradable, as if biodegradable paper were Vermilion's own scientific breakthrough. Still, the company actually did take steps to cut pollution at its paper mills even beyond state and federal air and water standards. It purchased the best new equipment and initiated research into new production methods that would reduce the amount of sulfites and chlorine used to make and bleach its paper.

So the new strategy was timely, disingenuous, and nevertheless real. Most executives cared more about the company's profits and image than about its environmental impact, but many saw the two as closely related and thought it ought to be possible to clean up operations enough to satisfy conscience and preserve Vermilion's good name in the marketplace without hurting dividends. There were even a few who believed that ways could be found to make paper profitably without polluting rivers or destroying ecologically valuable forests—and that it was the paper industry's responsibility to find them.

One of these was Peter Ostenson, director of offshore production, and it was offshore, especially in the Third World, that a genuine environmental policy would have its greatest impact. Vermilion expected its own pulp needs to grow some two million tons a year by the turn of the century, and tropical forests would inevitably provide much of the increase. The tropics were new to Vermilion, and Ostenson wanted to get off on the right foot. He was convinced that the environmental agenda and the business agenda had to come together to the benefit of both. Otherwise, they would collide to the detriment of both.

He had his work cut out for him selling this idea to top management. Oliver Hibbing, the president and CEO of Vermilion Paper, actively supported the so-called environmental strategy, but he made it clear to Ostenson that his first responsibility was to the stockholders.

"I'm a company man, Peter. So if you tell me we have to learn new ways of doing business because that's what our customers want, that's what we'll do. If I didn't buy that argument, I certainly wouldn't be spending all this money. But let somebody else run the environment. I'm with you on strategy—what more do you want?"

Ostenson always responded the same way. "It's a false distinction, Oliver. The company is *part* of the environment."

WITH RAIN FORESTS nearly as vast as those of Brazil or Indonesia, the nation of Equitania has a quarter of its 210 million acres of land in some type of forestry production. The country produces nearly 20% of the world's tropical hardwoods and supplies the wood for about two million tons of paper pulp annually. All told, forestry contributes some $2 billion annually in foreign exchange and is Equitania's second highest export earner. Japanese companies hold about half the foreign forestry concessions; the other half belongs to companies from South Korea, Malaysia, Thailand, Singapore, Hong Kong, and the Philippines.

In the mid-1980s, Vermilion Paper began exploring the possibility of starting a eucalyptus plantation in Equitania to help meet the company's growing pulp and paper needs. Ostenson and Hibbing calculated that by 1993, the venture would need to produce the raw material for about 500,000 tons of pulp per year at an estimated startup cost of roughly $350 million, plus $180 million for expansion of an existing pulp-and-paper mill in Indonesia to process Equitanian eucalyptus as it arrived by sea. On Ostenson's recommendation, they chose Wendell Buyck to set up an office in Palakra, the Equitanian capital, identify a site, and pursue Equitanian government approval.

Buyck had no foreign experience to speak of. What he did have, in addition to seven years' experience in Vermilion middle management and an undergraduate degree in forestry, was energy, intelligence, and determination. Even more important, he shared Ostenson's views about incorporating sound environmental principles into Vermilion's business agenda.

On setting up shop in Palakra, Buyck found a bewildering array of government agencies and regulations. He quickly saw that many of the regulations were absurd and some of the agencies dishonest, but with little knowledge of the country and no capacity for bribery, he realized that all he could do was play by the rules.

An official at the Ministry of Forests encouraged him. "Many of us would rather deal with Americans because they try to comply with the law. Most Asian companies do not even make the attempt," he said. "On the other hand, that is probably why Americans do poorly here."

With this ambiguous advice to go on, Buyck decided to seek full, formal government authorization for the project at every step rather than run the risk of government sanctions at a later date. Although government authorization would not prevent officials from invoking additional regulations—or demanding payoffs—in the future, it would improve his odds of building a viable project.

As a first step, Buyck complied with foreign-investment regulations by forming a joint venture between Vermilion and Ankora Corporation, an Equitanian conglomerate dealing mostly in minerals and construction. As president of the joint venture, called Veranko, Buyck applied to the government for permission to create a eucalyptus plantation. In hopes that his application would move faster and more smoothly if he made friends and contacts at the ministries, Buyck met personally with dozens of key officials.

After months of delays, the government granted Veranko a 35-year, 398,000-acre concession in the Keewa

Tinang province. Almost half of the land had recently been lumbered for hardwoods, and the foreign timber company involved had leveled the forest. This clear-cutting was an asset for Veranko. Buyck's plan to farm eucalyptus required open land, and Buyck had been looking for a recently logged parcel, partly so Veranko wouldn't have to cut any rain forest, partly for the satisfaction of reclaiming—and being seen to reclaim—deforested, despoiled land.

Government permit in hand, Buyck then turned his attention to nongovernmental bodies with stakes in the forest industry. The most powerful of these was Equitrass, the Equitanian Trade Association, a kind of self-appointed but quasi-official regulatory agency that enforced the rules of a dozen ministries—generously for member companies, harshly for others. While membership dues were modest, Equitrass also assessed large mandatory fees for its "production fund." Refusing to pay was tantamount to refusing to join, and refusing to join meant certain failure. Veranko chose to join and to make the production fund payments.

Buyck's next move was suggested by the experience of foreign companies in several nearby countries. In Indonesia, for example, the residents of one town ransacked and forced the closure of a Dutch-owned rubber plantation because the company had operated without community approval. In Malaysia, villagers revolted against logging in the rain forest even though the timber company had struck a deal with provincial leaders.

Suspecting that a concession from the government was not enough, Buyck decided that Veranko should seek approval directly from the local residents. Locating the plantation in Keewa Tinang increased the potential for problems because the Keewatinians resented the economic and political domination of the central government at Palakra, which they saw as little better than a colonialist power. They were also concerned about losing ultimate ownership rights to a foreign corporation and about the fate of their villages, lakes, and sacred tribal sites.

Buyck agreed to lease the land directly from the Keewatinians for a term of 35 years at a specified fee, in addition to the rent negotiated with the government in Palakra. He further assured local and provincial officials that he would keep the plantation away from villages, watersheds, lakes, and religious sites and that he would set aside the remaining rain forest in the concession as a nature preserve. Buyck also agreed to employ local people and to provide the province with a hospital, a school, and 100 kilometers of roads.

"He met our demands," recalls one community leader. "Other companies just come in and do whatever they want. Buyck was willing to listen."

Wendell Buyck had now spent nearly two years in Equitania. To Hibbing and the directors back in Michigan, progress seemed painfully slow. At this rate, the paper mill would come on line years behind the market opportunity. And now this man Buyck was agreeing to build schools and hospitals. Preserving virgin rain forest had the right sound to it, but schools and hospitals? Vermilion Paper was not a general contractor and certainly not a social service organization. These commitments might have some public relations value, but what about all those millions of paper towels that wouldn't be sold while Vermilion saved the world?

Peter Ostenson had to remind his superiors that Buyck was not trying to save the world, only Vermilion Paper. He took every opportunity to resell the environmental strategy to Hibbing, who still did not entirely buy Ostenson's contention that the time and money spent on this one project could pay a tenfold return in Third World goodwill, marketplace approval, and the increasingly well-publicized scorekeeping of environmentalists.

Ostenson himself began to wish that Buyck could move faster. But Buyck could smell victory on his own terms and was making no compromises. His next move was to conduct a six-month pilot study in the concession area to find a fast-growing species of eucalyptus. Of 109 varieties, Buyck chose one that would permit harvesting every five years, instead of the usual six to eight, which meant Veranko could grow more trees in less space.

The pilot study impressed the Equitanian government. "We would be in great shape if all companies were as thorough as Vermilion Paper," one official at the Ministry of Forests told Buyck.

Finally, Buyck began to address the concerns of Equitanian environmental groups, an unprecedented step for any foreign corporation. He asked the leaders of PELLONA, a consortium of more than 100 Equitanian environmental and community groups, for their advice on the Veranko project. Initially, PELLONA was unwilling to talk to Buyck because it feared alienating its own constituency. At the time, PELLONA was aligned with the international Vermilion Action campaign.

"Buyck was different, or at least he sounded different," recalls Maria Biwapik, PELLONA's director. "But we found it hard to believe that Vermilion had really changed its stripes. In fact, Buyck was a little too good to be true. Because he worked for Vermilion, we drew the obvious conclusion: he *wasn't* true. He was just Vermilion's way of getting its hands on that concession. Once it co-opted all the potential opposition, it would revert to business as usual—cutting rain forest, draining wetlands, ignoring the natives."

Buyck was undaunted by PELLONA's refusal to listen. He turned to the minister of environmental affairs—by now a friend—and asked him to set up a discussion between Veranko and PELLONA. After much urging and arm-twisting, PELLONA finally agreed to a meeting, but only after an internal struggle between PELLONA leadership and a group of dissenting member organizations led by MYP, a small, militant organization that opposed all further forest exploitation in Equitania. Since a closed meeting with Buyck would conjure up the awful specter of PELLONA getting into bed with the enemy, the meeting was to include delegates from at least a dozen PELLONA constituents, MYP among them. No one in PELLONA was taking any chances. In a meeting with deforesters, there had to be witnesses, consensus, and daylight.

Buyck opened the meeting by reading a statement picturing Veranko as a friend of the environment, supporting the concept of environmentally responsible development, and asking for a common effort to make such a strategy work—in effect a quid pro quo between business and environmental interests. Hackles rose. The MYP representative attacked Vermilion at length. Buyck backpedaled.

He said he was sorry if he had offended anyone and told them he needed their help. He then spoke passionately of his personal convictions. He told them how carefully and conscientiously he had satisfied the demands of government ministries. He described his negotiations with the tribal elders in Keewa Tinang, emphasizing the school and hospital. He made much of the pilot project. He underlined the fact that Veranko would plant only on land already cleared and would cut no new rain forest. He avoided any mention of resistance within his own company.

He did not succeed in allaying suspicions—dislike of Vermilion was too intense for that—but Maria Biwapik, for one, began to sense an opportunity. If Buyck meant even half of what he said, why not hold him to his word, seize him by his outstretched hand, and not let go? And why not use the opportunity to give PELLONA some valuable limelight?

She asked Buyck if he would sign a binding agreement limiting the size of the tree farm and guaranteeing the rain forest now within the concession as a permanent preserve. She also asked him to give PELLONA a permanent right of access and oversight. She rejected the idea of a quid pro quo but pointed out that PELLONA could hardly raise comprehensive objections to a plantation operated according to a plan that PELLONA itself had helped create and had the right to monitor.

Buyck blanched. He knew that Vermilion could not possibly yield anything approaching even token control of its operations to environmentalists, even if they had been a lot more friendly than PELLONA. He proposed a compromise. Veranko would hire PELLONA as a consultant to the project. He offered a fee of $20,000.

The MYP delegate called it blood money. Biwapik and the others wanted to know what guarantee they had that Veranko would follow their recommendations. "None," Buyck said. But what guarantee did they have now? He needed their advice, he said. His record demonstrated an honest desire to do right by the rain forest, by Equitania, and by the Keewatinians. He reminded them that he had asked for this meeting. He assured them that enlightened Vermilion leadership had come to believe—as this project made clear—that the paper industry could live in harmony with the environment.

It wasn't much, but it was more than Biwapik had expected. She actually found herself believing in Buyck's sincerity. The following day, the PELLONA steering committee held a long, heated meeting. No single delegate or member organization believed Vermilion could be trusted, but, like Biwapik, most instinctively trusted Buyck. Only the MYP delegate and one or two others held fast to the too-good-to-be-true theory and thought Buyck was actually lying.

In the end, the steering committee voted to accept the consulting assignment, refuse the fee, and take a position of guarded "nondisapproval" of the Veranko project. What that meant in practice, Maria later explained to Buyck on the phone, was that for the time being, PELLONA would refrain from condemning Veranko but would keep its options open. "That's all I ask," Buyck said. "But what about MYP?" Though she had her doubts, Maria assured him that MYP would consent.

In fact, MYP had voted loudly against any form of cooperation with Vermilion. But MYP was chronically short of money, and if it wanted to remain inside PELLONA and use PELLONA's resources, it would have to go along with the majority—or so Maria reasoned. Of course MYP had a point: Vermilion certainly wasn't to be trusted and had to be watched closely. But this could be the chance PELLONA had been waiting for to bring pressure to bear on other foreign companies and convince the government and Equitrass that a strict environmental policy could work. And if PELLONA could take some of the credit for a success in Keewa Tinang, which Buyck's arrangement would let it do, so much the better. She wasn't about to let MYP sabotage such a rich opportunity.

For his part, Buyck was immensely pleased and relieved. He knew Hibbing was close to abandoning the whole project out of sheer impatience. Now Ostenson could tell him the project had passed its last great hurdle. Detailed planning and construction could now proceed with the blessings of the Equitanian government, the trade association, the Keewatinian community, and, however guardedly, some of the very environmental groups that had been supporting the Vermilion Action campaign. Reason had won a victory over both greed and passion. The environmental strategy was going to be a success. Buyck and Ostenson were vindicated.

Six weeks later, the Forest Defense Legion—a militant U.S. environmental group with close, informal ties to the Equitanian MYP—ran in four major U.S. dailies a full-page ad condemning Vermilion.

The Forest Defense Legion held a press conference later the same day to announce that unless Vermilion cancelled its project in Keewa Tinang within 30 days, the FDL would organize a worldwide boycott of Vermilion products.

The following day, meetings were held in Equitania and Michigan. In Equitania, Maria Biwapik and the other members of the PELLONA steering committee considered ways of limiting the damage. If Vermilion canceled the project, that was the end of PELLONA's golden opportunity to play in a bigger league and convert its convictions into practice. But if PELLONA defended Vermilion Paper and urged it to stay, it risked the utter loss of its credibility with other environmentalists.

Maria and many of the others were furious with MYP. "Why in God's name did you have to pick Vermilion?" she demanded. "There are a dozen worse companies doing business in this country and a thousand worse projects. What were you thinking of?"

"Don't climb on that high horse with me," the man from MYP responded angrily. "Are you trying to tell me that once our backs are turned, they won't cut rain forest to raise their yield? You're naive. They're all run for profit, these companies, and we attack them where we can. Most of the others have no retail customers we can appeal to. Vermilion does. It's as simple as that."

"I'm afraid you're the one who's naive," Maria said. "Please tell me what other company is even going to make the effort to work with us after this? Not only have you thrown away our chance to influence this project and every other forest project still to come, now we're going to have the government and Equitrass on our backs as well."

She paused. "This could set back the cause of the rain forest by ten years," she said. "And it could ruin PELLONA."

In Michigan, the choices were equally stark. Ostenson wanted to fight. The sheer injustice of the accusations made him dizzy. Who were these people? Did they really mean to make it impossible to change?

"If we don't fight this," he argued, "we lose not only the concession but also the strategy. Aside from the fact that it's so damned unfair, it's a business mistake to cut and run."

But Hibbing was not interested. "Peter, I don't know what you and Buyck think you've been up to these past three years, but it sure as hell hasn't been a business agenda. How is it *possible* you didn't see this coming? You weren't born yesterday. Buyck's been playing footsy with every bleeding heart in the Far East, and now the whole thing's exploded in his hands. What did he expect?"

"No one could have predicted that this one little group would go nuclear on us. Buyck made a superhuman effort to work with those people, and I still think he was right. We have to stand behind him and Veranko or give up the pretense of having any strategy or vision beyond our own bottom line. We're on trial here. Canceling is an admission of guilt—and we're not guilty."

Hibbing was icily patient. "Millions and millions of people haven't seen these ads," he said. "And if we write off this fairly small investment, they never will. If we fight it, we're inviting a worldwide boycott that will make Vermilion Action look pale by comparison. We're only on trial if we choose to be. Justice, Peter, has no net present value."

"Okay, you're right. This is not a question of justice," Ostenson said. "But it's not a question of image either. It's a question of strategy, tactics. To protect this company over the long haul, we simply can't lose sight of the bigger issues."

Hibbing gave Ostenson a long, cold look. "Well, then, how about this for a bigger issue. If we fight this thing, the stockholders would be fully justified in getting rid of both of us. And then having us committed. Boycotts are a kind of lunacy, Peter, and—maybe you're right—a kind of politics. But I'm a businessman. What are you?"

Should Vermilion Fight or Fold?

Four experts in environmental strategy discuss the options.

Vermilion should face this challenge openly. It has a good record in Equitania; why not emphasize it?

Pieter Winsemius *is director of the Amsterdam office of McKinsey & Company and leads its worldwide environmental practice. He was the Netherlands' minister of environment from 1982 to 1986.*

MUCH LIKE INDIVIDUALS, organizations react to challenge in predictable ways. First comes denial of the problem; then anger; and finally, the search for a solution. Oliver Hibbing and Peter Ostenson should take heed. Even though Wendell Buyck would be justified in reacting this way, it would be counterproductive for him to do so. Vermilion executives may be hurt, but they must swallow their pride and refrain from calling "foul." They have to deal pragmatically with the problem at hand.

First and foremost, Ostenson must convince Hibbing to buy into his views on the environment. In doing so, Ostenson should abide by three principles.

- **Be responsive.** Vermilion should organize a response that stresses accountability. Hibbing, as chief executive officer, should take responsibility for Vermilion's actions. He must be open with the press and the public; outsiders have an uncanny instinct for detecting half-truths or escapism. A straightforward response will demonstrate that Vermilion takes the concerns of consumers and environmentalists seriously.

Vermilion has a pretty good record in Equitania; why not emphasize it? Hibbing could publicly offer, and confirm in large-scale advertisements, to conduct an environmental impact assessment—or even more appropriately in this case, a societal impact assessment. Hibbing can present this to PELLONA, the Forest Defense Legion, or any other group for scrutiny. Most important, he can eliminate many doubts with regard to self-serving sweetheart statements by asking a group of world-class experts to give a second opinion, again publicly. Given the amount of homework already done, this should be relatively easy and should deflate much of the challenge from the FDL and the MYP.

- **Learn from experience.** Clearly, Vermilion must review its internal procedures and take measures to prevent falling into this trap again. At the minimum, it should reassess its own personnel policies. People in pivotal positions must have both the will and the skill to deal with such crises. It is unfair and a waste of good resources to send an inexperienced young talent like Buyck on such an important and complicated mission. Considering the mistakes he made—offering payment to environmental groups for consulting services and trying to gain sympathy by distancing himself from his company—I find it amazing that Buyck survived as long as he did. Vermilion would have fared far better if Buyck were backed by strong nationals or, ideally, if Vermilion had educated and trained Equitanians to run this project.

This points to a weakness often found among even the largest multinationals: a lack of international management expertise amplified by an alarming degree of environmental naivete. Many companies are shocked when they encounter protests from activists who rarely forgive environmental "mishaps," especially ones caused by "foreigners." Vermilion should form an advisory board of international outside experts who will meet several times a year and will help keep the company on its toes. Vermilion should also consider appointing someone with a strong environmental background to its board of directors.

Finally, Vermilion should launch a full-scale investigation of the safety and environmental risks of all activities at all sites. Though costly, this is a doable exercise that provides a solid framework for creating action programs that reduce the risks associated with products, processes, and facilities. It enhances the organizational ability to deal with any remaining risks through environmental skill building, installing appropriate safety devices and information systems, and developing the expertise and procedures necessary for emergency management.

This operational assessment can be supported by an additional strategic focus attained through a policy impact assessment, which provides structured insight into the potential impact of new environmental policies in different countries. Contrary to popular belief, environmental policy tends to be quite predictable once one understands the underlying logic and the cultures of the players involved. By providing a window on the future, such an assessment can be a powerful tool in planning corporate strategic development.

- **Don't back down.** Above all, Vermilion should not retreat from the progress it has made toward a sounder environmental policy. As Peter Ostenson points out, that would be a business mistake. It would also send a negative signal to all Vermilion employees that could erode much of the environmental groundwork the company has laid in the last five years. And it would provide further "evidence" for the environmentalists' Vermilion Action campaign and would do little good for the company's own Green Vermilion campaign.

In the long run, Vermilion will need to find new sources for its pulp supply. Forest management in the Third World can benefit both the company and its host countries. The pulp and paper industry, with its vast consumption of natural resources and its highly visible presence in consumer products and household waste, must expect increasing environmental scrutiny from the public, from policymakers—even from employees, who want to be proud of the company they work for. The environment is no longer a side issue for only governments and environmentalists to worry about. No company can permit itself to live in disharmony with the environment.

Vermilion should not try to outtalk the Forest Defense Legion but should humbly build on the coalitions it has already established.

Anthony L. Andersen *is president and CEO of H.B. Fuller, a chemical products company headquartered in Saint Paul, Minnesota.*

VERMILION SHOULD MOVE forward with its plans in Equitania. As a global company with a growing need for pulp from outside the United States, it should be committed to making this test case a success. If it can't find the pulp in Equitania, it will have to find it elsewhere. And no matter where it goes, it will find conditions like those in Equitania.

Moreover, Vermilion's bad reputation will precede it. The Forest Defense Legion will see to that. Vermilion's marketing campaign to convince the public of its environmental soundness didn't cut the mustard with anybody for one simple reason: you can't just talk about doing something; you have to do it—and do it well over time.

For these reasons, Vermilion should not undertake a campaign against the FDL. The company cannot outtalk the group. Instead, it should humbly and strongly build the coalitions it has already begun. Vermilion should recognize this not as a short-term event but as part of a long-term strategic plan: the company needs pulp today and will need it tomorrow. It should move forward with these seven steps.

1. **Obtain an option to roll over the lease of the property beyond 35 years.** Go for 50 years. Go for 70, 100. The whole purpose of concern for the environment is long-term existence and balance. If Vermilion doesn't send a clear message of long-term commitment, it is not being honest with shareholders, environmental groups, or governments.

2. **Formalize the agreements with the federal government of Equitania and the provincial government of Keewa Tinang.** Establish that the terms are for the

full length of the lease—that there will be no changing the rules without mutual consent. This is not an inappropriate request: Weyerhauser and other paper companies that grow their own trees have 100-year plans for the use of resources.

3. **Convince Oliver Hibbing to "make his stand."** Hibbing is going to have to make a public stand on this issue or be booed out of office by investors or the board of directors. First, he needs to acknowledge that environmentalists have an important role to play in Vermilion's long-term strategy. Until he does this, the company will always be under pressure. Furthermore, Hibbing's involvement up front, both internally and externally, could make him a hero. He could come out of this positively received by all constituencies. In that sense, this confrontation represents an opportunity for Vermilion to make progress: dramatic situations call for dramatic actions. Hibbing must commit his full support or drop the whole initiative.

4. **Encourage the FDL to meet with and join PELLONA.** This will bring U.S. environmental groups into the process of monitoring Vermilion's operations in Equitania. This will also force the FDL to put up or shut up. It is going to be either part of the problem or part of the solution; this way, the FDL is part of the solution.

5. **Hold off on any board decision until the MYP and FDL are part of the project.** In other words, be vulnerable. Vermilion should open itself up and say that it won't make a decision until these groups are part of the process. Then if the MYP and FDL drag their feet, local governmental organizations will have a stake in

this issue, will worry about the loss of jobs, and so might actually pressure the groups to join the project. Moreover, Vermilion directors should be given the time to visit, observe, and make an informed decision. I would schedule the board meeting at least six months in advance so that the board perceives a real opportunity to make the right decision.

6. **Continue to build on the relationship with Maria Biwapik.** Credit her publicly for anything positive that comes along, and make it clear that Vermilion genuinely appreciates her efforts. Biwapik is taking quite a risk, and risk takers have to be encouraged.

7. **Take no action against the FDL for its newspaper ad.** Let the attack go unchallenged—no retaliatory ads or lawsuits. Don't inflame the conflict in the media: that's an impossible battle to win. Play it cool and defuse the emotion. If Vermilion challenges the FDL's claims, its past will come back to haunt the company.

   Vermilion will have to get along with the environmental groups for the length of the lease. If it starts the project in a confrontational way, some people might react emotionally and make it their objective never to give Vermilion any peace.

Vermilion needs to start thinking about the environment as an issue that won't go away.

Jacqueline Aloisi de Larderel *is director of the industry and environment office at the United Nations Environment Program in Paris. The views expressed here do not necessarily represent the policy statement of UNEP.*

THE PUBLIC MELTDOWN over the Equitanian project will force Vermilion to take at least one positive step: confront the fact that it has no overall environmental policy. Vermilion must stop reacting to external pressure on an ad hoc basis and begin to incorporate the environmental dimension in its long-term strategy. Until Vermilion does this, these crises will inevitably occur.

Vermilion's top management merely pays lip service to environmental concerns. Indeed, Oliver Hibbing's speeches show that the company does not value them at all. For all its hype, Vermilion has not incorporated environmental values into its decision-making process. It lacks even the most basic procedures or mechanisms to deal with environmental issues. It did not, for instance, subject the Veranko project to an environmental impact assessment—a tool that since the mid-1980s has been an effective way to assess potential environmental impacts and identify possible remedies. Nor does Vermilion value the ability to deal with environmental issues and related problems as a criterion in choosing its managers. The company provides no incentive to develop cleaner processes, while those who do take action—such as Wendell Buyck—are left without support.

Buyck's results are not as negative as they sound. He has initiated a successful dialogue with many of the partners, including the environmental groups. Yet despite his good and genuine intentions, Buyck was bound to fail without any true management support. He was unable to defend his statements picturing Vermilion as a friend of the environment because he had no credibility. He lacked the data to show both the environmental performance of Vermilion's operations in other parts of the world and the environmental impact of his project.

Buyck also failed because he doesn't have the proper skills and experience. He could have pushed the Equitrass negotiations as an opportunity to incorporate environmental principles into Vermilion's agenda. He never discussed a replantation or reforestation plan with the community, nor did he suggest organizing the training of local people in forestry. Finally, he contacted the environmental groups too late in the process.

Vermilion must start to follow through on its environmental claims. It cannot use marketing to address the environment—as it did when it launched an advertising campaign to tout the environmental investments it made only when activists began to apply pressure! As Sigvard Hoggren, a vice president of Volvo, has said, the most dangerous thing you can do is to look at your environmental ethics as a PR exercise: this won't work. The point is that it is the action that counts—not the hype. And not action merely in one plant but in the whole company. Vermilion needs to start thinking about the environment as an issue that won't go away. It needs to assess the environmental impact of the company's products, processes, and facilities. And it needs to translate its environmental values into practice—from training employees to deciding whether to use recycled or virgin pulp.

The Veranko joint venture should not be abandoned but be rethought in the framework of this new global policy. The Veranko case can be used to show Vermilion's willingness to change its policy. I would keep Buyck in the project: he has opened the dialogue, he has a good local image, and he believes in what he is doing. What he needs is backup. Vermilion should provide someone with experience who will help Buyck take advantage of the valuable work he has already done and the solid relationships Buyck has already built. Above all, the company should continue the important dialogues he has established—even with the Forest Defense Legion.

Vermilion should not shut down the project but continue moving forward at a slower pace. This is a long-term process that requires flexibility as the company learns how to implement its policy goals. The more immediate action Vermilion needs to take is the one it should have taken at the beginning of the process: to think through just how its overall environmental policy fits within its global company strategy and then design steps to make the policy work.

Environmental advocates have the responsibility both to criticize negligent companies and to support exemplary ones.

Jay D. Hair *is president of the National Wildlife Federation, a private, nonprofit conservation organization based in Washington, D.C.*

VERMILION HAS NO OPTION but to press on with its plans. The cost of forgoing this venture goes far beyond a negative return on investment: Peter Ostenson and Wendell Buyck have provided a rare and valuable blueprint for other corporations to follow in developing environmentally sound business strategies. If this experiment fails, the corporate and environmental communities will both be worse off for it.

Vermilion's problem is one of trust. Its reputation is a result of years of insensitivity to environmental concerns and will not be easy to change. The environmental community has learned from dealing with Vermilion that caution, wariness, and a healthy dose of skepticism are good qualities to have. So how can Vermilion change its image and gain the acceptance and cooperation of environmental groups? There are four strategic steps the company can take to build on the trust established by Ostenson and Buyck.

- **Avoid quick fixes.** Green cheer-leading without substance invites a backlash that will negate whatever environmental goodwill a company has shown. For Vermilion and other companies, justice may have no net present value, but corporate greenwash promises an equally dismal rate of return.
- **Implement progressive environmental protection programs.** Going above and beyond the call of regulatory duty is a sure way to gain the attention and respect of environmentalists. Companies will find them more willing to listen if environmental improvements are driven by culture rather than compliance.
- **Don't cut corners.** Buyck's meticulous efforts to involve all interest groups in the planning and development process have been instrumental in his successes so far. Community involvement and respect for cultural diversity are essential for any development game plan.
- **Recognize the expanded role of corporations in achieving sustainable economic development.** Environmental protection is the tip of the social policy iceberg. Buyck was right on target in trying to involve the company in local health and education improvement programs. Sustainable development involves more than just environmental protection. If Vermilion

ignores other critical social needs, the whole development effort is in danger of collapsing.

Overall, Vermilion should avoid two mistaken conclusions from this experience. First, the company may be tempted to pursue a divide-and-conquer strategy and take advantage of what it perceives to be a fragmented environmental front. This would be disastrous. There is diversity within the environmental community, just as there is diversity in any industry trade group. But as every biologist knows, diversity is a sign of health, vitality, and strength. Environmental groups have proven their effectiveness in working together and make a formidable team. Corporations electing to manage their environmental affairs by playing interest groups off each other are destined to fail.

The other, equally erroneous conclusion would be that the effort was a waste of time and that an anti-corporate bias will eventually doom any proactive measures Vermilion decides to pursue. The bottom line is that environmental groups do have responsibilities regarding their involvement with corporations. As environmental advocates, we have a responsibility to criticize companies that have been negligent in their environmental stewardship and to draw public attention to them. We also have an obligation to promote and support exemplary corporate environmental accomplishments. That means identifying positive actions a company may take to improve environmental quality and offering alternative solutions to problems when we believe the proposed options are not enough.

These principles are particularly relevant to Vermilion. The environmental community can be an important touchstone for industry in identifying issues of public concern and in establishing the trust and communication necessary for beneficial environmental practices. Nevertheless, there will always be some inherent conflict. Even if Vermilion sheds its old habits and follows a strategy of always "doing the right thing," it may face opposition from environmentalists in the future. Why? Because there will be occasions when the long-term ecological values at stake are so great that the best mitigation and contingency plans will not sufficiently address environmentalists' concerns.

Equitania, however, is not one of those situations. The clock is ticking. Oliver Hibbing should increase his visibility, take the offensive, and bring in the environmental, governmental, and public opinion leaders to participate in the development plan. He must demonstrate his personal and lasting commitment to Buyck's efforts. If the plan is as good as advertised, he will find a very receptive and helpful audience.

Originally published in May–June 1991
Reprint 91311

About the Contributors

STUART L. HART is a faculty member in corporate strategy and the director of the Corporate Environmental Management Program at the University of Michigan Business School in Ann Arbor.

PAUL HAWKEN is the founder of the Smith & Hawken retail and catalog company, cofounder of the knowledge-management software company Datafusion, and author of *The Ecology of Commerce* (HarperCollins, 1993).

JONATHAN LASH is president at the World Resources Institute, an environmental think tank based in Washington, D.C. The organization receives financial support from corporate foundations and companies, some of which are mentioned in this article.

CHARLES LOCKWOOD is an environmental and real estate consultant based in southern California and New York.

AMORY B. LOVINS is a former MacArthur Fellow and the research director and CFO of Rocky Mountain Institute (RMI), a nonprofit policy center.

L. HUNTER LOVINS is the CEO of Rocky Mountain Institute (RMI), a nonprofit policy center.

KIMBERLY O'NEILL PACKARD is a consultant with McKinsey & Company in Boston.

FOREST L. REINHARDT is the John D. Black Professor of Business Administration at Harvard Business School.

BILL SELLS was a manager and executive with Johns-Manville and the Manville Corporation, where he ended his career as a senior vice president and president of the Fiber Glass Group.

ALISSA J. STERN is founding director of International Dispute Resolution Associates, a nonprofit organization based in Washington, D.C., that specializes in helping companies and environmental organizations work more productively with one another.

FRED WELLINGTON is a senior financial analyst at the World Resources Institute, an environmental think tank based in Washington, D.C. The organization receives financial support from corporate foundations and companies, some of which are mentioned in this article.

Index